52 CELEBRATE & WORSHIP
Kids' Sermons and Object Talks

Gospel Light

How to Make Clean Copies from This Book

You may make copies of portions of this book with a clean conscience if

- you (or someone in your organization) are the original purchaser;

- you are using the copies you make for a noncommercial purpose (such as teaching or promoting your ministry) within your church or organization;

- you follow the instructions provided in this book.

However, it is ILLEGAL for you to make copies if

- you are using the material to promote, advertise or sell a product or service other than for ministry fund-raising;

- you are using the material in or on a product for sale; or

- you or your organization are not the original purchaser of this book.

By following these guidelines you help us keep our products affordable.

Thank you,

Gospel Light

Permission to make photocopies or to reproduce by any other mechanical or electronic means in whole or in part any designated* page, illustration or activity in this book is granted only to the original purchaser and is intended for noncommercial use within a church or other Christian organization. None of the material in this book may be reproduced for any commercial promotion, advertising or sale of a product or service. Sharing of the material in this book with other churches or organizations not owned or controlled by the original purchaser is also prohibited. All rights reserved.

*Pages with the following notation can be legally reproduced: © 2000 by Gospel Light. Permission to photocopy granted. *Celebrate and Worship*

Gospel Light

Editorial Staff

Publisher, William T. Greig

Senior Consulting Publisher, Dr. Elmer L. Towns

Publisher, Research, Planning and Development, Billie Baptiste

Managing Editor, Lynnette Pennings, M.A.

Senior Consulting Editors, Dr. Gary S. Greig, Wesley Haystead, M.S.Ed.

Senior Editor, Theological and Biblical Issues, Bayard Taylor, M.Div.

Editor, Sheryl Haystead

Editorial Team, Amanda Abbas, Mary Gross, Karen McGraw

Contributing Editor, Linda Mattia

Designer, Carolyn Henderson

Contents

Celebrate and Worship

Celebrate and Worship Overview

Welcome to a year's worth of celebration!

God's family always has the best reasons to rejoice: we know who God is and realize what He has done for us!

Celebrate and Worship will help you and your students discover how God's people—around the world and throughout time—have celebrated and still celebrate God's gifts to us. These discoveries contribute to meaningful and enthusiastic worship and praise to God for His greatness.

The Holidays

Celebrate and Worship incorporates holidays and celebrations from several sources:

- Hebrew holidays celebrated by God's people since Old Testament times,
- seasonal holidays and
- holidays taken from the church calendar.

Many of these holidays will be familiar to you and your students. Others will bring new opportunities to rejoice in God's goodness. These object talks give us an understanding of the vast scope of God's celebrations, spanning years and cultures to remind us of who He is and what He has done!

Included with the holiday celebrations are a number of object talks about various psalms. Each psalm has been chosen to help students learn about Bible-times worship customs while they celebrate a gift from God.

Hebrew Holidays

Old Testament holiday celebrations were designed by God Himself! And He designed them to be hands-on experiences reinforcing what He wanted to teach His people. For instance, God's instructions for celebrating the Feast of Tabernacles involve mind, voice, body and heart—each participating family builds a sukkah ("booth"), lives in it and participates in active praise and worship times before God. Could there be a more effective way to remember and retell the story of God's provision for His people during the years of wandering?

Hebrew holidays are very much like parables, for they reveal powerful spiritual truths. Many of us have missed this richness in our faith largely because we don't even know about these historic foundations. There is a wealth of understanding to be gained that can delight and surprise us with the way it completes our appreciation of God's work throughout history!

Seasonal Holidays

The seasonal holidays celebrated during this course are those that are most widely accepted and typically observed. Many countries and cultures celebrate these occasions in some form.

Church Holidays

Many of us already celebrate some church calendar holidays: Christmas and Easter, perhaps Advent and Lent. But this course will take us deeper into church history to teach us more of what God has done throughout history since Jesus' time on earth and how His family, both around the world and through time, has celebrated His goodness!

Psalms: The Music of Worship

The psalms were the heart and soul of celebratory expression for ancient Judaism. The psalms provided songs for the most joyous parties and the most solemn worship times. The goal of these object talks is to motivate children to worship God for who He is and what He has done for us. So it's appropriate that some psalms are also the central focus for the object talks, giving us more ways to understand how great our God is.

Expect a Celebration!

When you and your team members are full of eagerness and understanding of the object talk at hand, your students will be eager to learn and inspired by every celebration! As you pray and organize these object talks to meet the needs of your group, ask God for a sense of expectancy of what He wants to do during this time and for sensitivity to ways you can be part of what He desires to accomplish. Scripture tells us we'll be celebrating God's goodness throughout eternity. So let's get a start on it now!

Advice and Answers for Schedule Planning

Customizing the Holiday Schedule

Because these kid sermons and object talks focus on specific holidays and gifts of God, teachers have the unique opportunity to turn every object talk into a celebration! Here are some tips for making every object talk easy and effective.

The holidays are listed nearest the time when they normally are celebrated, beginning with those that occur in the fall. However, due to the undated nature of the material, minor adjustments may need to be made. As you look over the object talks, make a note beside each object talk as to this year's date for a given holiday. You may wish to switch object talks accordingly so that each holiday is celebrated on the day nearest its date that year. In a parent letter, explain what is being taught, when and why. List holiday dates, so parents know when those holidays will be the focus.

Your church may celebrate a particular holiday in a way or at a time slightly different from what is described in the object talks. For instance, there are differing dates for Transfiguration Sunday and varying colors of candles for Advent. Feel free to investigate these differences and include or substitute your church's way of celebrating the holiday.

Customizing the Object Talk Schedule

You may wish not to celebrate a holiday that appears in this book (Lent, for example). The object talk can be taught without mentioning the holiday at all; just adapt the conversation to highlight the celebration focus.

Not every object talk celebrates a holiday. On those days, the focus is on a gift of God that can be celebrated. Especially during the summer sessions, when there are fewer holidays, consider these ways to keep the celebration atmosphere fresh and exciting. Plan seasonal celebrations (such as a Sunshine Party, a Garden Party or a Water Party that include theme-related games and activities). Focus on the gift of God as the theme for celebrating (such as a Everybody's Birthday Party, a Talent Party or a Praise Party).

The Jewish Calendar

The Jewish calendar is a lunar calendar of 360 days a year, while much of the western world operates on a solar, 365-day calendar. Therefore, dates for a holiday on the lunar calendar vary considerably from year to year. (And remember, Jewish holidays always begin at sundown the night before the day they are usually marked on our calendars!)

Below is a chart that gives the approximate times of year for the biblically mandated feasts.

BIBLICAL MONTH	MODERN EQUIVALENT	FEAST NAME
Nisan	March/April	Unleavened Bread/ Passover
Iyar	April/May	
Sivan	May/June	Weeks/Pentecost
Tammuz	June/July	
Av	July/August	
Elul	August/September	
Tishri	September/October	Trumpets (Rosh Hoshanah) Day of Atonement (Yom Kippur) Tabernacles (Sukkot)
Heshvan	October/November	
Kislev	November/December	Dedication (Hanukkah)
Tevet	December/January	
Shevat	January/February	
Adar	February/March	Purim

Kid Sermon and Object Talk

TIPS

Object talks can draw children in and help them understand our reasons for celebrating. These object talks can be used as children's sermons or used to supplement any Sunday School curriculum. They can also be used to augment any children's ministry program, day school or home school curriculum.

Getting the Most Out of a Kid Sermon and Object Talk

Preparation is the key to using *Celebrate and Worship!* Read a talk at least several days ahead to give ample time to gather the needed materials. You may find it helpful to practice some talks before presenting them.

Whenever possible, invite children to participate. Each week ask a different child to read the Bible verse aloud (highlight the verse in your Bible and mark its location with a bookmark).

Occasionally describe situations in which knowing about the meanings behind the celebrations has helped you. Tell children how the Bible verse presented in the lesson has been important to you.

When the object talk is about one of the psalms, involve children in reading that psalm aloud as a choral speaking activity. Invite them to use rhythm instruments, create clapping patterns or do actions based on the words of the psalm. Many of the psalms used in *Celebrate and Worship* are available in music form on the *God's People Celebrate* cassette/CD and music video. During the object talk you may also wish to play one of the songs, inviting children to sing along and/or do the actions shown in the *God's People Celebrate* music video for that psalm.

Using a Kid Sermon and Object Talk During Adult Worship

If the children in your church are in the adult service during the first part of the service, consider using the object talk as the basis for a weekly children's sermon. Introduce the idea of the object talks in *Celebrate and Worship* to the adult audience by saying, **This year our children are learning all about reasons to celebrate God's gifts to us. Today they will be studying ___.** Give the talk and then, if possible, ask one or more of the Discussion Questions found in bold print at the end of each talk.

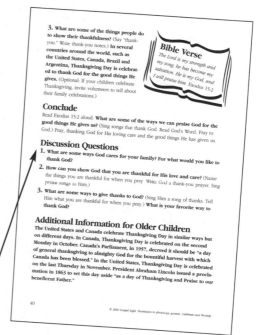

Helping Kids Make the Transition to Adult Worship

For a few moments, let's do a little pretending. Let's pretend that we are six-year-old children and that we are sitting in the adult worship service of our church. What words will we hear that we don't understand? What books are we asked to use that we don't know how to read? What happens in front that we can't see because we are small? What are we expected to do that is confusing to us? How long do we have to sit still when we are not used to sitting?

As you think through some of the things your children experience in a typical worship service, you may come to the realization that the adult worship service sometimes becomes an uncomfortable, passive experience for a child rather than an opportunity to praise and worship God.

However, you as a children's program leader, as well as parents, pastor and others involved in leading the adult worship service, CAN take many specific actions to make the service more meaningful and enjoyable for children. Whether the children in your church are approaching the first time they will attend the service, attend the service only occasionally, frequently attend at least part of the service or are about to be promoted from their own children's church program into regular attendance at the adult worship service, here are some specific suggestions to help them enjoy and benefit from being with the grown-ups in "Big Church."

When Children Are in the Worship Service

Encourage parents to sit with their children near the front of the worship service. They will not only see and hear better, but they will also have more of a sense that the person up front is speaking to them. Proximity encourages participation.

Arrange for those who are involved in leading worship to meet periodically with the children in fairly small groups. This can be done briefly at the end of Sunday School or as a part of another children's program. Use this time to explain one feature of the service the children are about to attend. If this is done every week or on some other regularly scheduled basis, the children can gradually be introduced to the entire spectrum of worship activities which occur in your services.

A significant bonus of this approach is that children will also get to know your leaders as friends who care about them, rather than viewing them as strangers who lead unfamiliar ceremonies at a distance. Perhaps of even greater significance, this brief time of interaction will alert these leaders to the presence of children in the worship service, helping the leaders become more effective in including children in the worship experiences.

HINT: If you invite someone to meet with the children and this person is not experienced in speaking at a child's level, structure the time as an interview which one of the children's teachers or leaders will conduct. Let your invited guest know ahead of time the specific questions that will be asked.

Provide parents with a sheet of tips of things to have the child do before, during and after the service in order to gain maximum understanding and participation (see next page).

12

Tips for Parents

Before the Service:

• Sit near the front where your child can easily see what is happening.

• If your church prints an order of service in the bulletin, help your child identify, find and mark locations of hymns and Scripture readings.

• Let your child underline all the words in the bulletin he or she can read.

• Briefly explain the meaning of any difficult words or phrases in at least the first hymn you will sing.

• Share your own feelings about the hymns or songs to be sung: "This is one of my favorites," "I really like to sing this because it helps me tell God I love Him," "This is one I've never learned—I hope it's easy to sing," etc.

During the Service:

• Let your child help hold the hymnal or song sheet. Run your finger beneath the words being sung to help your child follow along. If your church displays the words of each song on an overhead, make sure you sit where your child can see the words.

• Touch your child (not just when the wiggles are in action) to build a sense of warmth in being together.

• Provide writing and/or drawing materials. Encourage your child to write or draw about things he or she sees or hears during the service ("Draw a picture of something the pastor talks about in his sermon.").

• If there is a time to greet one another, introduce your child to those around you.

• Let your child take part in passing the offering plate, registration cards or other items distributed throughout the congregation.

After the Service:

• Express your appreciation at being in church with the child.

• Commend your child for specific times when he or she was participating well ("You really did a good job singing that first hymn.").

• Talk about what went on in the service. Avoid making this sound like an exam, but ask one or two questions to let the child know that you expect him or her to be listening. A few good questions to use are "What is one thing you remember from the service?" "Which song did you like best?" "What Bible person did the pastor talk about?" and "What was the pastor trying to teach us about?"

• Share your own answers to those questions, or let your child ask you any questions he or she desires.

• Explain one or two things that happened in the service that you think your child was interested in or could have been confused by.

Tips for the Children's Program Leader

As the children's program leader, you can also take specific actions to make the adult worship service more meaningful to the child. Look at everything that is done through a "six-year-old's filter." Ask yourself, *What would a child understand from what we just did?* This is not a plea to conduct six-year-old-level worship services, but it will help adults become aware of children's presence and their right to be led in meaningful worship of the Lord. The child will not understand EVERYTHING that occurs in every service, but the child deserves to understand SOMETHING in every service.

Meet with the person(s) responsible for planning the worship service and talk about ways to make the service more helpful to children. Consider these ideas:

Worship Room

• Choose at least one hymn or song with a repeating chorus, which makes it easier for children to learn and participate.

• Choose at least one hymn or song with fairly simple words and melody.

• Introduce at least some hymns with a brief explanation for children.

• Once or twice in the service mention, "Our children are worshiping with us and we want to help them know what we are singing (talking) about." This will help raise the congregation's aware-ness of their responsibility to guide children and will also explain some things to adults and teenagers that they might be embarrassed to ask about.

• Provide simple explanations of special observances (baptism, the Lord's Supper, etc.).

• When inviting people to greet one another, remind them to include children in their interac-tion. Instructions such as "Talk to at least one person from a generation other than your own" or "Greet someone who is now attending school" are enjoyable ways to alert adults without making the children feel put on the spot.

• Find ways to involve children in some specific aspects of the service. Many churches are familiar with occasionally having a children's choir sing, but often the children feel more like outside performers than participants in family worship. Occasionally invite children to assist in receiving the offering (perhaps have parent-child teams), handing out bulletins, reading

14

Scripture, answering a question, etc. Some churches periodically give their choir the day off and form a family choir with moms, dads and kids singing a simple song with other families after a brief rehearsal or two.

• If the adults in your congregation wear name tags, provide name tags for the children to wear as well.

• Provide clipboards, paper and crayons for children to use during the service. Before the sermon, the person leading the service can suggest that the children listen for a particular person or event during the sermon and draw a picture about that person or event on the paper. Children may pick up the clipboards during a hymn or some other appropriate time just before the sermon.

• Make a checklist of things for the children to listen for during the service. As the children hear one of the things listed, they check it off the list.

• Several months before children are promoted from their children's church program into regular attendance at the adult worship service, plan to have the children participate in a portion of each service each week or the entire service once a month.

• Ask a person with video equipment to make a recording of the entire worship service. Then, occasionally choose specific parts of the service to show and explain.

• If the order of worship is printed in your bulletin, give each child a bulletin and briefly explain the order of worship. Describe in childlike terms how each part of the service helps us worship God.

• If your congregation sings a song often (such as the "Doxology" or "Gloria Patri"), teach it to the children. You may also help them become familiar with the Lord's Prayer or the Apostles' Creed (if they are used in your church) by repeating them from time to time in your program.

• Help children understand that worship is anything we do that shows that we love and respect God. Use your conversation to help your children understand how praise, music, prayer and learning from God's Word are all important aspects of worship.

Leading a Child to Christ

One of the greatest privileges of serving in children's programs is to help children become members of God's family. Some children, especially those from Christian homes, may be ready to believe in Jesus Christ as their Savior earlier than others. Ask God to prepare the children to receive the good news about Jesus and prepare you to communicate effectively with them.

Talk individually with children. Something as important as a child's personal relationship with Jesus Christ can be handled more effectively one-on-one than in a group. A child needs to respond individually to the call of God's love. This response needs to be a genuine response to God—not because the child wants to please peers, parents or you, the leader.

Follow these basic steps in talking simply with children about how to become members of God's family. The evangelism booklet *God Loves You* is an effective guide to follow. Show the child what God says in His Word. Ask the questions suggested to encourage thinking and comprehending.

1. God wants you to become His child. (See John 1:12.) **Do you know why God wants you in His family?** (See 1 John 4:8.)

2. You and all the people in the world have done wrong things. (See Romans 3:23.) **The Bible word for doing wrong is "sin." What do you think should happen to us when we sin?** (See Romans 6:23.)

3. God loves you so much He sent His Son to die on the cross for your sins. Because Jesus never sinned, He is the only One who can take the punishment for your sins. (See 1 Corinthians 15:3; 1 John 4:14.) **The Bible tells us that God raised Jesus from the dead and that He is alive forever.**

4. Are you sorry for your sins? Do you believe Jesus died to be your Savior? If you do believe and you are sorry for your sins, God forgives all your sins. (See 1 John 1:9.)

When you talk to God, tell Him that you believe He gave His Son, Jesus Christ, to take your punishment. Also tell God you are sorry for your sins. Tell Him that He is a great and wonderful God. It is easy to talk to God. He is ready to listen. What you are going to tell Him is something He has been waiting to hear.

5. The Bible says that when you believe in Jesus, God's Son, you receive God's gift of eternal life. This gift makes you a child of God. This means God is with you now and forever. (See John 3:16.)

Give your pastor the names of those who make decisions to become members of God's family. Encourage the child to tell his or her family about the decision. Children who make decisions need follow-up to help them grow in Christ.

NOTE: The Bible uses many terms and images to express the concept of salvation. Children often do not understand or may develop misconceptions about these terms, especially terms that are highly symbolic. (Remember the trouble Nicodemus, a respected teacher, had in trying to understand the meaning of being "born again"?) Many people talk with children about "asking Jesus into your heart." The literal-minded child is likely to develop strange ideas from the imagery of those words. The idea of being a child of God (see John 1:12) is perhaps the simplest portrayal the New Testament provides.

A Sweet New Year

God's forgiveness is for everyone who believes in Jesus.

Celebration

Feast of Trumpets, Rosh Hashanah

Scripture Background

Leviticus 23:23-25; Numbers 29:1-6

Bible Verse

Everyone who believes in him receives forgiveness of sins through his name. Acts 10:43

Teacher Materials

Bible with bookmark at Acts 10:43, apples, knife, bowls, lemon juice, honey, napkins.

Prepare the Activity

Slice apples and place slices in bowls. Drizzle apple slices with lemon juice to prevent browning. Pour approximately ⅓ cup honey into bowls. (Prepare one bowl of slices and one bowl of honey for every six to eight children.)

Introduce the Object Talk

No matter how old or young we are or how many good or bad things we've done, we can receive God's forgiveness when we believe in Jesus. Since Bible times, God's people (called Hebrews, or Jews) have celebrated a holiday that reminds them of their need for forgiveness. This holiday is called the Feast of Trumpets.

Present the Object Talk

1. **The Feast of Trumpets got its name because it began with the sounds of a trumpet, called a *shofar* (SHOH-fahr) in Bible times.** (Optional: Older children read Leviticus 23:23,24.) **This holiday was the beginning of a time of year when God wanted His people to turn away from their sins—the wrong things they had done. This was a time to realize that they needed God's forgiveness for their wrong actions.**

2. Rosh Hashanah (RAHSH huh-SHAH-nuh) is another name for this celebration; it means "new year." The Hebrew calendar started a new year in the fall. Rosh Hashanah reminds people to start the new year by celebrating God's loving forgiveness. To celebrate the new year, special foods are eaten. What are some special foods you eat at parties or celebrations? (Birthday cake. Thanksgiving turkey.) **Apples dipped in honey are eaten at Rosh Hashanah to show that a sweet or good new year is hoped for.** Children dip apple slices into honey before eating.

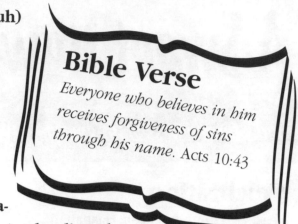

Bible Verse

Everyone who believes in him receives forgiveness of sins through his name. Acts 10:43

Conclude

Apples and honey remind us that God gives us many good things. God's greatest gift is that when people believe in Jesus and admit their sin, God forgives them. Read Acts 10:43 aloud. Thank God for His forgiveness. Talk with interested children about becoming members of God's family (see "Leading a Child to Christ" on pp. 16-17).

Discussion Questions

1. What are some things people might think they have to do to be forgiven? (Go to church. Read their Bibles.) **Those are all good things to do, but who does Acts 10:43 say can have their sins forgiven?** (Anyone who asks God for forgiveness of sin and who believes in Jesus.)

2. What does it mean to believe in Jesus? (To believe that Jesus is God's Son and that He died to take the punishment for our sins.)

3. How can we be sure our sins are forgiven? (God always keeps His promises.)

Additional Information for Older Children

In the Old Testament book of Micah we can read about God's forgiveness of sin. Ask a volunteer to read Micah 7:18,19. **How do these verses describe God's forgiveness of sin? As a reminder that God takes away all sin, on Rosh Hashanah Jewish people throw bread crumbs into the ocean or a river and watch the crumbs disappear.**

Shofar Sounds

God's forgiveness helps us make a new start.

Celebration

Feast of Trumpets, Rosh Hashanah

Scripture Background

Leviticus 23:23-25; Numbers 29:1-6

Teacher Materials

Bible with marker at 2 Corinthians 5:17;
optional—*shofar,* trumpet, horn, or prerecorded
trumpet sounds (see pattern below) and player;
rhythm instruments.

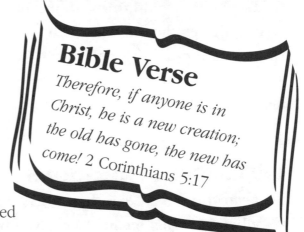

Bible Verse

Therefore, if anyone is in Christ, he is a new creation; the old has gone, the new has come! 2 Corinthians 5:17

Introduce the Object Talk

When we believe in Jesus, God's forgiveness helps us make a brand-new start. God forgives the wrong things we have done. In the Old Testament the sound of a trumpet reminded the people of their need for forgiveness. Let's find out what happened.

Present the Object Talk

1. (Optional: Play blasts of *shofar* or trumpet.) **When do you hear trumpets blow?** (Parades. Concerts. Church.) **In Bible times, God's people played trumpets as signals. On the holiday called Feast of Trumpets, the sound of a trumpet called a *shofar* signaled the people to remember their need for God's forgiveness. *Shofars* were made from the horns of rams.**

2. At the Feast of Trumpets, also called Rosh Hashanah (RAHSH huh-SHAH-nuh), the *shofar* is played in a special way. Clap hands in this pattern: one clap followed by a long pause, three claps, nine fast and short claps, one clap. Invite children to clap hands in this same pattern, repeating the pattern several times.

(Optional: Blow pattern on *shofar* or any single note of trumpet or horn or play prerecorded trumpet sounds. Children play pattern with rhythm instruments.)

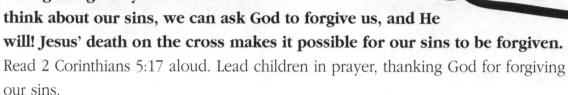

Conclude

In Bible times at the Feast of Trumpets, God's people would think about the wrong things they had done. When we think about our sins, we can ask God to forgive us, and He will! Jesus' death on the cross makes it possible for our sins to be forgiven. Read 2 Corinthians 5:17 aloud. Lead children in prayer, thanking God for forgiving our sins.

Discussion Questions

1. **According to 2 Corinthians 5:17, "the old has gone and the new has come"; what does this mean?** (When you become a member of God's family, you don't have to feel guilty for the wrong things you have done. You have a new chance to obey God and do right things without worrying about the past.)

2. **When are some times that kids your age need to ask forgiveness?**

3. **How do we know God forgives us?** (He sent Jesus to take the punishment for our sin. God promises to forgive us when we are sorry for what we have done and ask for His forgiveness.)

Additional Information for Older Children

The sound of the trumpets not only signaled a time to get ready for the forgiveness of their sins but also signaled a new year was beginning. (In Bible times, the people didn't have calendars to keep track of what day of the week or year it was.) The words "Rosh Hashanah" actually mean "new year." When do we celebrate the beginning of the new year? (New Year's Eve in the month of December.) **Find out the season of the year in which the Hebrew people in Bible times celebrated their new year.** Children read Leviticus 23:23-25 to find information: the Hebrew people's seventh month which is the fall of our year—the months of September or October.

"Awe"some Forgiveness

God's forgiveness of our sins helps us forgive others, even when they don't deserve it.

Celebration
Days of Awe

Scripture Background
Psalm 139:23,24

Teacher Materials
Bible with bookmarks at Psalm 139:23,24 and Ephesians 4:32; large sheet of paper; marker.

Bible Verse
Be kind and compassionate to one another, forgiving each other, just as in Christ God forgave you. Ephesians 4:32

Prepare the Object Talk
Print several misspelled words and incorrect math problems on large sheet of paper, adjusting the difficulty of the spelling and math according to the age of your children.

Introduce the Object Talk
Because God forgives us when we ask, we can forgive others, even when they don't ask! In Old Testament times, there were 10 days during which God especially wanted His people to carefully think about the sins for which they needed to be forgiven. Let's find out about these 10 days and what it means to carefully look for something wrong.

Present the Object Talk
1. The 10 days between the Feast of Trumpets and the Day of Atonement are now called the Days of Awe. What do you think of when you hear the word "awe"? (Awesome. Things that are very good or beautiful.) **The word "awe" means those things, but it also means respect, admiration and amazement. During the Days of Awe, as God's people thought about how wonderful and perfect God**

is, they also thought about their own lives and realized the wrong things they had said and done.

2. Show paper you prepared. Invite volunteers to correct the spelling and math. **In order to find what was wrong with these words and problems, we looked carefully for what was wrong. In the same way, during the Days of Awe, people examined their actions so that they knew what sins to ask forgiveness for.**

3. When we believe in Jesus and become members of God's family, we are forgiven once and for all—forever! But the Bible says we should still look carefully at our lives and make sure they are pleasing to God. Read, or ask a child to read, Psalm 139:23,24.

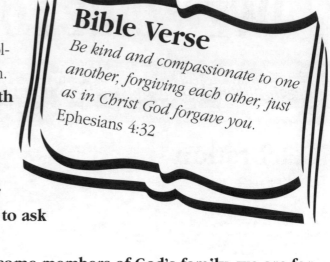

Bible Verse

Be kind and compassionate to one another, forgiving each other, just as in Christ God forgave you.
Ephesians 4:32

Conclude

Knowing we are forgiven should make us want to please God more and more. Being forgiven makes us want to do something else. Read Ephesians 4:32 aloud. **What does God's forgiveness help us want to do?** (Forgive others.) Pray, thanking God that when we ask, He forgives our sins and helps us want to forgive others.

Discussion Questions

1. When can kids your age forgive others? (When others cheat you or lie to you.)

2. What can we do to show forgiveness? (Say I forgive you. Smile. Be friendly.)

3. Why does God's forgiveness help us forgive others, even if they don't deserve it? (God forgives us, even when we don't deserve it. To show our thankfulness to God, we show His love to others by forgiving them.)

Additional Information for Older Children

Invite several older children to take turns reading these verses that describe God's forgiveness and love: Psalm 103:1-4,8-13.

At One with God

Jesus' death on the cross made it possible for us to be saved through the forgiveness of our sins.

Celebration

Day of Atonement, Yom Kippur

Scripture Background

Leviticus 16; 23:26-32; Numbers 29:7-11

Teacher Materials

Bible with bookmark at 1 Timothy 2:3,4; variety of objects used to cover things (tablecloths, blankets, slipcovers, hats, coats, canopy, box or pan lids, umbrellas, etc.).

Bible Verse

God our Savior . . . wants all men to be saved and to come to a knowledge of the truth.
1 Timothy 2:3,4

Introduce the Object Talk

God loves us so much that He planned a way for our sins to be forgiven. In Bible times, on a special day called the Day of Atonement, the priests followed God's instructions for forgiveness. Let's find out what happened on the Day of Atonement and how we can be sure that our sins are forgiven.

Present the Object Talk

1. Show each object you brought. **What is this object used for?** After all objects have been shown, ask, **What do all of these objects have in common?** (They are all used to cover something.) Ask children to name other coverings.

2. The Hebrew name for the Day of Atonement is Yom Kippur (YAHM kih-POOR) which means "day of covering." When something is completely covered up, you can't see it. It's like the object doesn't exist. That's how it can be with our sins—the wrong things we have done. Even though the first people

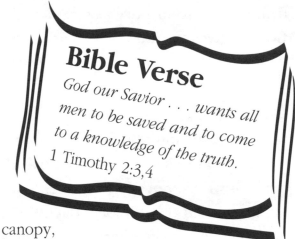

who celebrated the Day of Atonement didn't know about Jesus, today we can believe that Jesus is God's Son and that He died on the cross to take the punishment for our sins. Then we become members of God's family. When God looks at us, He doesn't see our sins—they are not only covered up by Jesus' death, but our sins are also removed. God forgives us and our sins are gone! God promises that He will NEVER remember them again!

Conclude

Because Jesus took the punishment for our sins by dying on the cross, we say that Jesus atoned for our sins. Instead of being separated from God by our sins, our sins are removed. Now we can be "at one" with Him. So no matter what name you call this holiday, Day of Atonement, or Yom Kippur, the good news for everyone everywhere is that our sins are forgiven. Read 1 Timothy 2:3,4 aloud. Pray, thanking God for sending Jesus to die on the cross so that our sins can be forgiven. Talk with interested children about becoming members of God's family (see "Leading a Child to Christ" on pp. 16-17).

Discussion Questions

1. **How can we stop doing wrong things?** (Ask God to forgive our sin and to help us do what's right.)

2. **How do we know that our sin is forgiven?** (The Bible tells us that if we ask God for forgiveness for the wrong things we have done, we will be forgiven.)

3. **What are some ways we can learn the right things God wants us to do?** (Read God's Word. Follow the instructions of people who love God. Pray.)

Additional Information for Older Children

A scapegoat is something or someone blamed when things go wrong. That word comes from something that happened on the Day of Atonement. Ask a child to read Leviticus 16:10. On the Day of Atonement the high priest would ask God to put all the blame for everyone's sins onto a goat. Then the goat was chased away into the desert never to be seen again to show that God had removed the guilt of the people's sins for another year.

Debt Free

When we realize how much we have been forgiven, we become more willing to forgive others.

Celebration

Jubilee

Scripture Background

Leviticus 25:8-55; 27:17-24

Teacher Materials

Bible with bookmark at Luke 6:37, a variety of household bills.

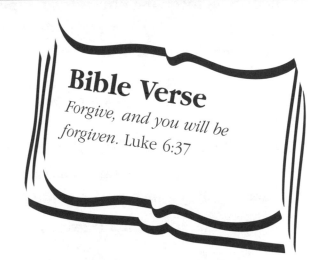

Bible Verse

Forgive, and you will be forgiven. Luke 6:37

Introduce the Object Talk

Because God has forgiven us, we are to forgive others, too! In Bible times, God's people celebrated a holiday that reminds us how important it is to forgive others. This holiday, called the Year of Jubilee, was celebrated once every 50 years! Let's find out what happened in this holiday.

Present the Object Talk

1. Show children the bills you brought and make a comment such as, **When I get bills like these, it means I have to pay someone for the gasoline I've put in my car and for the electricity and water I've used in my house. Until I've paid these bills, I'm in debt, which means I owe money. How do you think I would feel if someone told me I didn't have to pay these bills?** (Excited. Happy. Glad.)

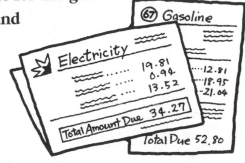

2. During the Year of Jubilee if you owed someone money, your debt was taken away, or forgiven. Slaves were set free! And if you had sold land to someone, that land would be returned to you. God wanted His people to celebrate the Year of Jubilee so that poor people would

receive the help they needed. The word "jubilee" means liberty or freedom. This holiday was celebrated the whole year long! (Optional: Older children read Leviticus 25:10; 27:24.)

Bible Verse

Forgive, and you will be forgiven. Luke 6:37

Conclude

God thinks forgiving others is so important that He doesn't want us to do it only once every 50 years. Read Luke 6:37 aloud. **The Bible teaches us that because God has forgiven us, He wants us to forgive others every day.** Pray, thanking God for His forgiveness and asking His help in forgiving others.

Discussion Questions

1. In what ways do people today show that they forgive others? (Treat the person kindly. Be friendly. Say "I forgive you.")

2. When has someone forgiven you? How did you know you were forgiven?

Additional Information for Older Children

Jesus made it very clear that He places a high priority on forgiveness of others. Read Jesus' story of a forgiving king in Matthew 18:21-35.

Branches of Praise

God gives us everything we need.

Celebration
Feast of Tabernacles, Sukkot

Scripture Background
Exodus 23:16; Leviticus 23:33-36,39-43

Teacher Materials
Bible with bookmark at Philippians 4:19, several tree branches; optional—one or more objects used at sporting events (pom-pom, pennant, foam hand, etc.).

Bible Verse
My God will meet all your needs according to his glorious riches in Christ Jesus.
Philippians 4:19

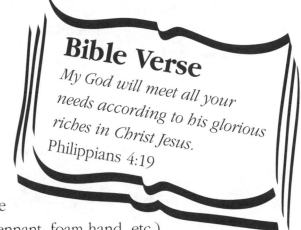

Introduce the Object Talk
It's important to remember all that God has done for us. In the Old Testament God's people celebrated the Feast of Tabernacles to help them remember how God took care of them when they left Egypt. Let's find out some of the things they used in this celebration and how the celebration got its name.

Present the Object Talk
1. Show branches. **At the Feast of Tabernacles, called Sukkot (suh-KOHT) in Hebrew, God told His people to gather different types of tree branches and fruit.** (Optional: Read Leviticus 23:40 aloud.) **The branches and fruit were used in several ways. One way was to decorate small booths the people built. Traditionally, the people lived in these booths for the seven days of the celebration. Living in the booths reminded them of the time after they escaped from Egypt when they had no houses to live in. The word "sukkot" means booths or tabernacles, and that's why this celebration was called the Feast of Tabernacles.** (Optional: Read Leviticus 23:42 aloud.) **Even today Jewish people build and decorate booths as part of this holiday.**

2. Besides being used to decorate the booths, the branches were used to show praise to God. **What are some objects people use to cheer for or praise a sports team?** Volunteers tell. (Optional: Display objects used at sporting events.) Invite volunteers to wave branches (or hands) in the following traditional pattern for Sukkot: to the front, sides, back, up and down. **The branches were waved in all directions to show that God is ruler over all the earth.**

Bible Verse
My God will meet all your needs according to his glorious riches in Christ Jesus.
Philippians 4:19

Conclude

We can praise God, too, not just at the Feast of Tabernacles, but all year long. Read Philippians 4:19 aloud. **What does this verse tell us about God?** Volunteers answer. **This verse tells us a good reason to celebrate!** Pray, thanking God for giving us all that we need.

Discussion Questions

1. **What are some times in the Bible when God gave people what they needed?** (Manna and water to the Israelites in the desert. A dry sea for the Israelites to get away from Pharaoh. Instructions for Noah to build an ark, so he could be safe during the flood.)

2. **With the things God has given us, how can He use us to help provide for other people's needs?** (Share what you have with people who need it. Help serve food to people at a homeless shelter. Give offering at church, so the church can use the money to help people with their needs.)

3. **In what ways can you thank God for giving you everything you need?** (Pray. Tell others about His gifts. Sing songs of praise to God.)

Additional Information for Older Children

Traditionally, branches from three trees—myrtle, willow and palm—were collected at the Feast of Tabernacles. (Optional: Show one or more of the named branches.) **The branches were braided together and then waved in the air as a way of praising God. A fruit—called a citron—was also held and waved. A citron looks like a lemon.** (Optional: Show lemon.) **In Hebrew, the branches were called a** *lulav* **(LOO-lahv) and the fruit was called the** *etrog* **(EH-trog).**

30

Delicious Decorations

Remembering God's goodness throughout our lives makes us want to celebrate the ways He cares for us.

Celebration

Feast of Tabernacles, Sukkot

Scripture Background

Exodus 23:16; Leviticus 23:33-36,39-43; Deuteronomy 16:13-15

Teacher Materials

Bible with bookmark at Romans 8:28, several types of fruits and vegetables, large bag, one or more blindfolds, knife.

Prepare the Activity

Place fruits and vegetables in large bag.

Bible Verse

We know that in all things God works for the good of those who love him. Romans 8:28

Introduce the Object Talk

When we remember God's goodness throughout our lives, we want to celebrate His care. During Old Testament times God's people celebrated the Feast of Tabernacles, called Sukkot (suh-KOHT) in Hebrew, as a reminder of the good things God provides for His people. Let's discover some of the things they used in their celebration.

Present the Object Talk

1. What did the people build during the Feast of Tabernacles? Why? (God's people built booths to remind them of God's care for their ancestors while they traveled in the desert on their way to the Promised Land.) **Try to discover what items people in our city might use to decorate a booth during the Feast of Tabernacles.**

2. Blindfold one or more volunteers. Take out one fruit or vegetable from bag. Volunteer(s) tries to identify the food only by touching it. If volunteer(s) cannot identify food by touching it, suggest volunteer(s) smell and then taste bite-size pieces of the food. As time allows, repeat with new volunteers for each fruit and vegetable. **During Sukkot, the booths are decorated with fruits and vegetables as a reminder of the good things God provides for His people.** (Optional: Read Deuteronomy 16:13-15 aloud.)

Bible Verse
We know that in all things God works for the good of those who love him. Romans 8:28

Conclude

Fruits and vegetables are only a few of the good things God has given to His people. Read Romans 8:28 aloud. **This verse tells us that God always cares for us no matter what happens. What are some of the ways God has cared for you?** Pray, thanking God for the things mentioned in student responses. Close prayer by praising God for His goodness to us.

Discussion Questions

1. What are some ways to celebrate God's goodness? (Thank Him when you pray. Treat others with the same goodness God shows to you. Tell people about God's goodness. Sing songs of praise to Him.)

2. What does God show us about Himself by caring for us? (He loves us. He is good.)

3. How does God show His goodness to us in hard times? (Keeps His promises to us.)

4. What are some of the ways people today celebrate God's care? (Thank Him in prayer. Make banners or write prayers about God's care.)

Additional Information for Older Children

The Feast of Tabernacles was one of three important holidays God instructed His people to celebrate. In Bible times, God's people (called Hebrews, or Israelites) traveled to Jerusalem for these three celebrations. As they traveled, they sang songs from the book of Psalms. Psalms 120—134 are called the Psalms of Ascent. The word "ascent" means to be rising or climbing up toward something. Invite volunteers to read aloud the first verse of Psalms 120, 121, 122 and 123.

Signs of Change

Celebration
Reformation Day

Scripture Background
Hebrews 10:19-22

Teacher Materials
Bible with bookmark at Ephesians 2:8,9; a variety of signs or flyers (For Sale, Beware of Dog, No Trespassing, advertising flyers, etc.).

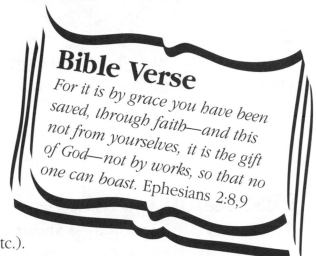

Bible Verse

For it is by grace you have been saved, through faith—and this not from yourselves, it is the gift of God—not by works, so that no one can boast. Ephesians 2:8,9

Introduce the Object Talk
Because God's love for us is so great, He wants us to accept His free gift of salvation. A long time ago, a man named Martin Luther wanted to make sure everyone heard the good news about salvation. Let's find out what he did.

Present the Object Talk
1. One at a time, display and discuss the various signs you brought. **What does this sign tell you?** Volunteers answer. Explain signs as needed.

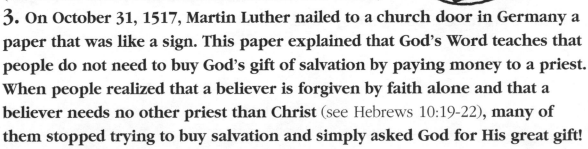

2. Signs help people by giving them information they need. What are some other ways to give people information? (Television. Radio. Bulletin boards. Internet and e-mail.)

3. On October 31, 1517, Martin Luther nailed to a church door in Germany a paper that was like a sign. This paper explained that God's Word teaches that people do not need to buy God's gift of salvation by paying money to a priest. When people realized that a believer is forgiven by faith alone and that a believer needs no other priest than Christ (see Hebrews 10:19-22)**, many of them stopped trying to buy salvation and simply asked God for His great gift!**

Today many people remember Martin Luther's actions on a day called Reformation Day. "Reformation" means to improve something, or to make right something that has been wrong.

Conclude

Read Ephesians 2:8,9 aloud. **What do these verses say God gives us?** (Salvation.) **What does it mean to have faith?** (To trust and believe that God's Word is true and that Jesus died and rose again to pay for our sins.) Pray, thanking God for His free gift of salvation through Jesus. Talk with interested children about becoming members of God's family (see "Leading a Child to Christ" on pp. 16-17).

Discussion Questions

1. **Grace is love and kindness shown to someone who doesn't deserve it. What does Ephesians 2:8,9 say about grace?** (We are saved because of God's grace.)

2. **Why can't we boast or brag about being saved?** (We are only saved when we believe in Jesus' death for our sins, not because of any good actions we have done.)

3. **Why is salvation described as a gift from God?** (It is free. There is nothing we can do to earn it. He gives it to us because He loves us.)

Additional Information for Older Children

Martin Luther's writings spread quickly. Here's why: Although Martin Luther wrote his paper in Latin, which many people didn't understand, his writing was later translated into German, a language that most people in his country understood. Then, many people were able to read his writings.

About the same time, the printing press was invented by Johann Gutenberg in a nearby town. Thousands of copies of Luther's writings were printed. These copies were given out all over Europe. The good news of God's free gift of salvation traveled all over Europe and beyond!

Faithful Heroes

Remembering the actions of people in God's family encourages us to show our faith in God.

Celebration

All Saints' Day

Scripture Background

Hebrews 11—12:1

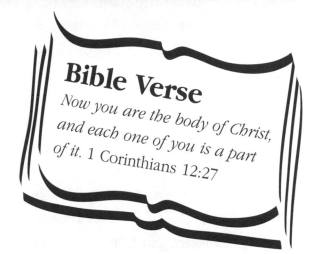

Bible Verse

Now you are the body of Christ, and each one of you is a part of it. 1 Corinthians 12:27

Teacher Materials

Bible with bookmark at 1 Corinthians 12:27, a variety of objects that remind us of other people (photo album, scrapbook, yearbook, postage stamp, locket, family Bible, coin, dollar bill, etc.).

Introduce the Object Talk

Members of God's family have done many things that are important for us to remember. Their actions of faith encourage us to show our faith in God, too. Let's talk about ways to remember what other people have done.

Present the Object Talk

1. Who is an important person in your life? What is something you could do to always remember that person? Volunteers respond. Display objects one at a time and discuss with children. **What is this object? How does an object like this remind you about people?** (Photographs, lockets and family Bibles remind us of our family and friends. Postage stamps, coins and dollar bills remind us of famous people and our country's leaders.)

2. A long time ago, Christians chose one day on which they would remember the people in God's family who had been hurt or killed because of their faith

in God and were already with Him in heaven. This special day is called All Saints' Day. The Bible calls anyone who believes in God and loves and obeys Him a saint. **What are people like who love and obey God? What kinds of things might they do?** Volunteers tell ideas. **On All Saints' Day, we remember and celebrate all the members of God's family who have lived before us and who have showed their great faith in God—even people from Bible times! Who are some Bible people you have heard about?** Children answer. (Optional: Older children read Hebrews 11 and make a list of the people of faith listed there. Children then share the list with the group.)

> ### Bible Verse
> *Now you are the body of Christ, and each one of you is a part of it. 1 Corinthians 12:27*

Conclude

We can celebrate and thank God that we are part of this family of faith! Read 1 Corinthians 12:27 aloud. **Another name for all the members of God's family is "the body of Christ." Just like every part of your body is important, every person in the body of Christ is important. Remembering how other people in God's family obeyed and followed Him helps us show our faith in God, too.** Pray, thanking God for all the members of His family and for the help of the Holy Spirit to obey God.

Discussion Questions

1. **What stories about Bible people help you want to love and obey God?**

2. **How can kids your age show faith in God?** (Do what God says in the Bible. Pray to God and ask His help in loving Him and others.)

3. **Who is someone you know who loves and obeys God? What can you learn about how to obey God from that person's example?** (Learn to tell the truth. Learn to be patient.)

4. **What are some ways kids your age can be examples of ways to love and obey God?**

Additional Information for Older Children

All Saints' Day is traditionally celebrated on November 1. The day before is called Halloween. The word "hallow" means holy or sacred. So "Hallow's Eve," or "Halloween," originally meant the evening of holy persons. Over the centuries, however, that meaning has been lost by many people.

Offering It All

Our offerings of love, time, abilities and money are ways we show our thankfulness to God.

Celebration
Offerings

Scripture Background
Leviticus 1:1,2; 2:1,2; 3:1

Teacher Materials
Bible with bookmark at 1 Chronicles 16:29, objects used by your church to collect offerings (boxes, bags, plates, tithe envelopes, banks, etc.), large bag, blindfold.

> ### Bible Verse
> Ascribe to the Lord the glory due his name. Bring an offering and come before him; worship the Lord. 1 Chronicles 16:29

Prepare the Activity
Place in bag objects used to collect offerings.

Introduce the Object Talk
An offering is anything we give to show love for God. We can give offerings of love, time, abilities and money to show our thankfulness to God. In the Old Testament, people gave many different types of offerings to God, too. Let's look at different ways to give to God.

Present the Object Talk
1. Invite a volunteer to wear a blindfold. Then take one object from the bag, hand it to blindfolded volunteer and ask him or her to identify the object. **What is this object used for?** Volunteer responds. Repeat, using a different volunteer for each object.
2. We use all these objects in our church to collect offerings. Explain use of objects to children as needed. **What are some other ways people give to show**

their love and thankfulness to God? (Bring canned foods. Give used clothes. Volunteer time to help or teach others at church. Sing in the choir.)

3. In Old Testament times, people gave different kinds of offerings, too. They gave animals, grains, oil, fruit and vegetables. God's people brought their offerings to the Tabernacle and later to the Temple— the places where the people gathered to worship God. The offerings were burned at a special place called an altar. These offerings were called sacrifices. (Optional: Read, or ask an older child to read, Leviticus 1:1,2; 2:1,2; 3:1 aloud.) **Some of the offerings showed God that the people were sorry for sinning; others showed that they wanted to love and obey God and were thankful for His good gifts to them.**

Conclude

The Bible tells us to give offerings to God. Read 1 Chronicles 16:29 aloud. **Unlike people in Old Testament times, we don't have to make offerings because of sin. Jesus died and rose again for ALL our sins. His sacrifice was the most important offering ever. Now we bring offerings to show our praise to God.** Pray, thanking God for the good things He gives us.

Discussion Questions

1. What kinds of offerings can you give to God? (Money. Time helping others. Love for God and others. Singing songs of praise.)

2. What attitude should we have when we give offerings to God? (An attitude of thankfulness. A happy and willing attitude that shows we are glad to give to God because we love Him and want to help the people He loves.)

3. When have you or your family given money or other things you own to show thankfulness to God? (Given books to a missionary family. Given money to church to help other people learn about God.)

4. Why is it important to give offerings to God? (Helps us remember God's gifts to us.)

Additional Information for Older Children

Provide several children's Bible dictionaries or encyclopedias. Invite children to read information about the different types of offerings described in the Old Testament: burnt offerings, grain offerings, fellowship offerings, sin offerings and guilt offerings.

Cornucopia of Thanks

Give thanks to God for His care for us.

Celebration
Thanksgiving

Scripture Background
Exodus 14,15

Teacher Materials
Bible with bookmark at Exodus 15:2, cornucopia or large basket, magazine pictures of good
things God has given us (food, family, friends, church, parks,
school, nature items—one picture for each child, including several examples from
each category).

Bible Verse

The Lord is my strength and my song; he has become my salvation. He is my God, and I will praise him. Exodus 15:2

Prepare the Activity
Place pictures in cornucopia or large basket.

Introduce the Object Talk
**As we learn about God, we discover the many wonderful ways He cares
for us. God's care for us is something we can celebrate and thank
Him for! Let's find out some of the gifts He gives us.**

Present the Object Talk
1. Ask a volunteer to take a picture from the cornucopia or basket, identifying the picture for the entire
group. **What is one thing about this picture
that makes you want to thank God?** Repeat,
using a different volunteer for each picture in the
cornucopia or basket.
2. At your signal, children group themselves into categories
according to their pictures. Repeat as time allows, having children select new pictures.

3. What are some of the things people do to show their thankfulness? (Say "thank-you." Write thank-you notes.) **In several countries around the world, such as the United States, Canada, Brazil and Argentina, Thanksgiving Day is celebrated to thank God for the good things He gives.** (Optional: If your children celebrate Thanksgiving, invite volunteers to tell about their family celebrations.)

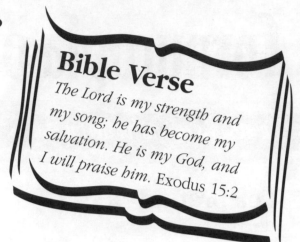

Bible Verse

The Lord is my strength and my song; he has become my salvation. He is my God, and I will praise him. Exodus 15:2

Conclude

Read Exodus 15:2 aloud. **What are some of the ways we can praise God for the good things He gives us?** (Sing songs that thank God. Read God's Word. Pray to God.) Pray, thanking God for His loving care and the good things He has given us.

Discussion Questions

1. What are some ways God cares for your family? For what would you like to thank God?

2. How can you show God that you are thankful for His love and care? (Name the things you are thankful for when you pray. Write God a thank-you prayer. Sing praise songs to Him.)

3. What are some ways to give thanks to God? (Sing Him a song of thanks. Tell Him what you are thankful for when you pray.) **What is your favorite way to thank God?**

Additional Information for Older Children

The United States and Canada celebrate Thanksgiving Day in similar ways but on different days. In Canada, Thanksgiving Day is celebrated on the second Monday in October. Canada's Parliament, in 1957, decreed it should be "a day of general thanksgiving to almighty God for the bountiful harvest with which Canada has been blessed." In the United States, Thanksgiving Day is celebrated on the last Thursday in November. President Abraham Lincoln issued a proclamation in 1863 to set this day aside "as a day of Thanksgiving and Praise to our beneficent Father."

Foreign Phrases

Because Jesus is God's Son, we can worship Him as King now and forever.

Celebration
Christ the King Sunday

Scripture Background
Philippians 2:9-11

Teacher Materials
Bible with bookmark at Zechariah 14:9, large sheet of paper, marker, world map or globe.

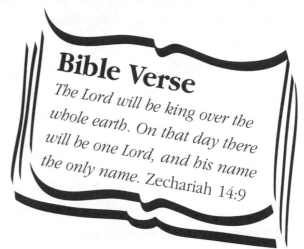

Bible Verse

The Lord will be king over the whole earth. On that day there will be one Lord, and his name the only name. Zechariah 14:9

Prepare the Activity
On large sheet of paper, print the following language names and phrases—English: Jesus is Lord; Spanish: *Jesús es Señor* (HAY-soos ehs sch-NYOHR); French: *Jesus est le Seigneur* (JHAY-soo eh leh seh-NYOOR); Tagalog (Philippines): *Si Hesus ay Panginoon* (SEH hay-SOOS ay PAH-nee-nah-ahn); German: *Jesus ist Herr* (YAY-soos eest HEHR); Italian: *Il Jesus é il Signore* (EEL HAY-soos eh eel seeg-NOH-ree). Practice saying the phrases.

Introduce the Object Talk
People all over the world can praise and worship Jesus. One way to worship Jesus is by celebrating a special day called Christ the King Sunday. On this day, Christians all over the world worship Jesus as King of heaven and earth for all time. Let's find out what some of these Christians might say to worship Jesus.

Present the Object Talk
1. The Bible tells us that one day, everybody on the earth will say that Jesus is Lord. Lord is a special name for Jesus that shows He is Ruler or King of all things and of all people. (Optional: Read Philippians 2:9-11

aloud.) **At our church, we speak (English) when we say ("Jesus is Lord").** Show map or globe and point out the area where your church is located.

2. People in each country of the world say these words in their own languages. Show paper you prepared with "Jesus is Lord" written in several languages. **This is how people say "Jesus is Lord" in (Spanish).** Repeat for each language, including languages spoken by the children in your group. On map or globe, find locations where each language is spoken as you help children pronounce the phrases.

> **Bible Verse**
> The Lord will be king over the whole earth. On that day there will be one Lord, and his name the only name. Zechariah 14:9

Conclude

Read Zechariah 14:9. **This verse talks about the day when Jesus returns to earth. Then everyone will understand that Jesus really is the King. How would you explain to a friend what this verse means?** Volunteers tell ideas. Close in prayer, inviting children to call out "Jesus is Lord" in any of the languages written on large sheet of paper.

Discussion Questions

1. What does it mean to say that Jesus is our King? (We want to love and obey Him. He is our ruler.)

2. When can we worship Jesus as King? (When we pray. When we sing songs of praise. When we talk about Jesus to others.)

3. Why is it important to worship Jesus? (To show our love to Him. To help others worship Him, too.)

4. What can we do to show that we believe Jesus is King and worship Him? (Obey what the Bible, His Word, tells us to do. Sing songs of praise to Him. Give Him offerings of love, time and money.)

Additional Information for Older Children

Kings or leaders of countries sometimes gain power because they lead their armies into war. Jesus' war was not against people or countries but against sin, death and God's enemy, Satan. By dying on the cross and rising from the dead, Jesus won the war against all the sin in the world. The Bible tells us that one day all people will recognize that Jesus is the King of kings.

Light of the Menorah

Come together to worship God for His power and protection.

Celebration

Feast of Dedication, Hanukkah, Festival of Lights

Scripture Background

John 10:22,23

Teacher Materials

Bible with bookmark at Psalm 18:2, a variety of candles (birthday cake candles, decorative candles, votive candles, etc.), menorah (or nine candles and candlesticks), matches.

Bible Verse

The Lord is my rock, my fortress and my deliverer; my God is my rock, in whom I take refuge. He is my shield and the horn of my salvation, my stronghold. Psalm 18:2

Introduce the Object Talk

God's power and protection are great reasons to come together and worship Him. In New Testament times God's people worshiped Him at a holiday called the Feast of Dedication. Today we call this holiday Hanukkah (HAH-nih-kah). Let's find out how this holiday started and what was done to celebrate it.

Present the Object Talk

1. Show different candles one at a time. (Optional: Light candles.) **How is this type of candle used?** Volunteers answer.

2. Show menorah (or nine candles and candlesticks). **This is called a Hanukkah menorah. Many years ago, God's people used a menorah in the Temple in Jerusalem. The Temple was where God's people came to worship Him. But in between the time of the Old Testament and the coming of Jesus in the New Testament, a Greek ruler who hated God did many wrong things in the Temple. The menorah was not lit for many years.**

After a group of Israelites defeated the army of this general, the religious leaders of the Israelites wanted to dedicate the Temple so that they could worship God in the Temple again. To dedicate something means to set it apart for a special purpose. The menorah was lit as part of the dedication of the Temple.

3. To remember God's power, Hanukkah, which is the Hebrew word for dedication, is celebrated for eight days. The Hanukkah menorah is a symbol of that celebration. Each day one candle is lit. Light the candles, using the middle candle to light them from left to right. When Jesus lived on earth, this holiday was celebrated by the Jews as a reminder of God's power in helping His people defeat their enemies. (Optional: Read John 10:22,23 aloud.)

Conclude

Read Psalm 18:2. **What does this verse say about God's power?** Pray, thanking God for His power to help and His protection from harm.

Discussion Questions

1. **What stories about God's power have you read in the Bible?** (The parting of the Red Sea. Elijah being fed by ravens. Jesus healing the blind man.)

2. **Why is it good to know about God's power?** (We can be sure of His help when we need it. We know we can depend on Him.)

3. **When have you been helped by God's power? How has God cared for you?**

4. **How do you need God's help and care today?**

Additional Information for Older Children

Hanukkah is sometimes called the Festival of Lights. This name not only reminds people of the lighted candles on the menorah but also of a story that was told about the relighting of the menorah. In Bible times, the branches of the menorah held oil, not candles. The story is told that there was found only enough oil for the menorah to burn for one day. However, the menorah continued to burn for eight days until more oil was made. God's people said that it was God's power that kept the menorah burning.

Ready Wreaths

Get ready to celebrate the birth of the promised Savior.

Scripture Background

Isaiah 9:1-7

Teacher Materials

Bible with bookmark at Isaiah 9:6, Advent wreath and candles; optional—picture of Advent wreath, matches.

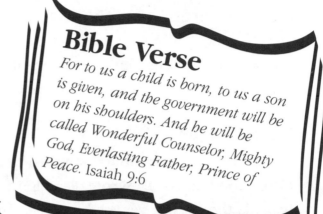

Bible Verse

For to us a child is born, to us a son is given, and the government will be on his shoulders. And he will be called Wonderful Counselor, Mighty God, Everlasting Father, Prince of Peace. Isaiah 9:6

Introduce the Object Talk

At this time of year, we're getting ready to celebrate the birthday of Jesus, the Savior sent by God. One word that describes this time of year means the same as "arrival" or "coming." Let's find out what this celebration is.

Present the Object Talk

1. What are some ways your family gets ready to celebrate Jesus' birth? Volunteers answer. **A word that some people use when they talk about getting ready to celebrate Jesus' birth is the word "Advent." Advent not only describes the season of the year in which we celebrate Jesus' birth, but it also describes four Sundays before Christmas when we can especially look forward or get ready to celebrate Christmas.**

2. Show Advent wreath. (Optional: Show picture of Advent wreath.) **On the first Sunday of Advent only the first candle is lit.** (Optional: Light candles as you describe them.) **The first candle is called the Hope candle. It reminds us of Old Testament times when**

God's people hoped and waited for the Savior God had promised to send. On each of the following Sundays, another candle is lit. The second, or Peace candle, reminds us of the peace Jesus gives us. The third, or Joy candle, reminds

us of the joy we feel at Jesus' birth. The fourth, or Love candle, reminds us of God's love for us and our love for God. Sometimes a fifth candle, called the Christ candle, is placed in the center of the Advent wreath. It is lit on Christmas Eve or Christmas Day to remind us of Jesus' birth. (Optional: As each candle is explained, invite volunteers to suggest a motion for the name of each candle. Ask children to describe other objects used at Advent—calendars, daily Advent candle, etc.)

Bible Verse

For to us a child is born, to us a son is given, and the government will be on his shoulders. And he will be called Wonderful Counselor, Mighty God, Everlasting Father, Prince of Peace. Isaiah 9:6

Conclude

The prophet Isaiah looked forward to the coming of God's promised Savior. Listen to what Isaiah wrote. Read Isaiah 9:6 aloud. **This verse reminds us that Jesus is the reason we celebrate!** Pray, thanking God for His love and for sending His Son, Jesus.

Discussion Questions

1. **Who was the promised Savior the Old Testament prophets told about?** (Jesus.)

2. **What do you do to get ready for school? to go on a trip? to celebrate Christmas? What do you do that especially reminds you of Jesus' birth?**

3. **Because Jesus came to live on earth, what do we learn about God?** (God loves all people. God made a way for our sins to be forgiven.)

4. **Who has helped you learn about the coming of Jesus as our Savior?**

Additional Information for Older Children

What colors of candles have you seen in Advent wreaths? Children tell. **Three purple candles are sometimes used in Advent wreaths to remind us of God's royalty. A pink or rose candle may be used for the Joy candle. The Christ candle is usually white and reminds us that Jesus is the light of the world.**

Advent not only celebrates Jesus' birth and the first time He came to earth, but it's also a time to look forward to His return! (Optional: Read Acts 1:9-11.)

Magnificent Music

We can worship God for His love and His promise to send the Savior.

Scripture Background

Luke 1:46-56

Teacher Materials

Bible with bookmark at Luke 1:46-56, rhythm sticks or other rhythm instrument; optional— recording of "The Magnificat" and player.

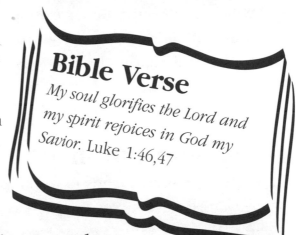

Bible Verse

My soul glorifies the Lord and my spirit rejoices in God my Savior. Luke 1:46,47

Introduce the Object Talk

God's love and His promise to send a Savior are good reasons to worship Him! Singing is one important way people worship God. Let's find out about one of the oldest songs ever sung about Jesus' birth.

Present the Object Talk

1. What are some songs that people sing at Christmas? ("Silent Night," "Jingle Bells," "Away in a Manger," etc.) Use rhythm sticks or other rhythm instrument to play the rhythms to several Christmas songs. Ask children to guess the names of the songs. (Optional: Lead children in singing one or more of the songs.)

2. All of these songs are sung at Christmastime, but the very first Christmas song was sung by Mary after the angel told her she was going to be Jesus' mother. The words of Mary's song are now part of a song called "The Magnificat" (mahg-NEE-fee-kaht), which is a Latin word. "The Magnificat" is sung in many churches, not just at Christmastime, but all year long. It is said to have been set to music more often than any other hymn! Read, or ask several children to take turns reading, Luke 1:46,47. (Optional: Also read verses 48-50 and/or play a portion of "The Magnificat.")

3. What did Mary praise God for in this song? (For being her

Savior. For doing great things for her. For His mercy.) **How is this song the same or different from the other Christmas songs we named?** Volunteers respond.

Bible Verse

My soul glorifies the Lord and my spirit rejoices in God my Savior. Luke 1:46,47

Conclude

The word "magnificat" means "to magnify." When we magnify God, we are praising Him and telling others how wonderful He is. Pray, praising God for His wonderful gift of His Son, Jesus. Talk with interested children about becoming members of God's family (see "Leading a Child to Christ" on pp. 16-17).

Discussion Questions

1. **What are some reasons to worship and thank God at Christmastime?** (He showed His love by sending Jesus as our Savior. He promised a Savior for many years.)

2. **What are some ways to worship God at Christmastime?** (Thank God in prayer and song for sending Jesus. Show God's love to others by giving gifts. Put up decorations that are reminders of Jesus' birth.)

3. **What is one way you would like to worship God this week?**

4. **How does giving and receiving gifts help us celebrate Jesus' birth?** (Jesus is God's gift to us.)

Additional Information for Older Children

Mary's song of praise is similar to a song sung by Hannah in the Old Testament. Mary sang her song to praise God for the great things He had done for His people and for loving her and allowing her to be the mother of Jesus, the Savior of the world. In a similar way, Hannah was praising God for giving her a son, Samuel, who would be dedicated to God's work. Children read some or all of Hannah's song in 1 Samuel 2:1-10.

Worldwide Praise

The birth of God's Son, Jesus, the Savior, is reason for the whole world to celebrate.

Celebration

Christmas

Scripture Background

Luke 2:1-20

Teacher Materials

Bible with bookmark at 1 John 4:9, nativity scene; optional—Christmas object from your cultural heritage.

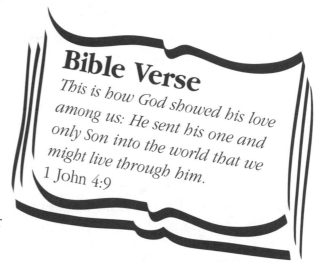

Bible Verse

This is how God showed his love among us: He sent his one and only Son into the world that we might live through him.

1 John 4:9

Introduce the Object Talk

The birth of God's Son, Jesus, is reason for everyone to celebrate. Many of our Christmas traditions, or the ways we celebrate Jesus' birth, actually began in other countries. Let's find out how one Christmas tradition began.

Present the Object Talk

1. What do you know about the place where Jesus was born? Volunteers respond. Display nativity scene. **One of the objects we often see at Christmastime is a nativity scene like this one. People all over the world put up nativity scenes at Christmas to remind them of Jesus' birth.**

2. Nativity scenes were first made in Italy about 800 years ago. Since then, people in countries all over the world make nativity scenes. In France, the nativity scene is used in place of a Christmas tree. In South America, a whole room is often dec-

orated as a nativity scene, including drawings of hills, shepherds, the wise

men crossing the desert and even sailboats on the sea! (Optional: Show object from your cultural heritage and explain its history and the customs surrounding it.)

Conclude

Nativity scenes are just one of the objects people all over the world use to celebrate the birth of God's Son, Jesus. Read 1 John 4:9 aloud. **What does this verse tell us is the reason God sent His Son to earth?** (God loves us.) Pray, thanking God for the gift of His Son, Jesus, and that we can celebrate Jesus' birth with people all over the world.

Bible Verse

This is how God showed his love among us: He sent his one and only Son into the world that we might live through him. 1 John 4:9

Discussion Questions

1. **Why should the whole world celebrate Jesus' birth?** (He came as the Savior for all people. God showed His love for the whole world when He sent Jesus.)

2. **What are some ways you've seen or heard the Christmas story?**

3. **What are some ways you, your family or our church tell other people that Jesus has been born?**

4. **What are some ways we can help others celebrate Jesus' birth?** (Send Christmas cards picturing events from the story of Jesus' birth. Sing praise songs about Jesus.)

Additional Information for Older Children

Most nativity scenes show the wise men worshiping Jesus at the stable. However, many people who study the Bible believe that the wise men actually arrived in Bethlehem when Jesus was between one and two years old. There are two reasons for this belief. First, it probably took the wise men a while to research the meaning of the star they saw, then to organize for their journey and then to travel a long distance. Second, when they arrived in Bethlehem, the Bible says they found Jesus in a house, not a stable. Read Matthew 2:11.

Wise Ways

Celebration

New Year's Eve and New Year's Day

Scripture Background

Proverbs 10:8,12; 12:18; 15:1; 17:17

Teacher Materials

Bible with bookmark at Proverbs 2:6, variety of lists (grocery list, phone book, chore list, encyclopedia, dictionary, etc.); optional—large sheet of paper, marker.

Bible Verse
For the Lord gives wisdom, and from his mouth come knowledge and understanding.
Proverbs 2:6

Introduce the Object Talk

If we ask God, He will give us wisdom to know the best way to live. When people celebrate the coming of a new year, they often think about better ways to live. Let's talk about how some people remind themselves of wise ways to live.

Present the Object Talk

1. Give each list you brought to a volunteer to describe. **What kind of list is this? How does this list help the person who wrote it or who is reading it? What kinds of lists do you or the people in your family make?** Volunteers respond.

2. As part of their New Year's Day celebrations, some people make lists called New Year's resolutions. A resolution is something you plan or promise to do. When people write New Year's resolutions, they usually list wise ways

of living. (Optional: Ask children to tell items often listed as New Year's resolutions.)

3. We can always think of good ways to live, such as eating healthy food or getting enough sleep, but because God loves us so much, He gives us the help we need to live the very best way. What are some ways we can find out the very best ways to live? (Ask God for wisdom. Read God's Word. Listen to advice from people who love and obey God.) Volunteers read Proverbs 10:8; 10:12; 12:18; 15:1 and 17:17 for additional ideas. (Optional: On large sheet of paper, children list wise ways to live that each begin with one of the letters in the words "Happy New Year.")

Bible Verse

For the Lord gives wisdom, and from his mouth come knowledge and understanding.
Proverbs 2:6

Conclude

Read Proverbs 2:6 aloud. **What are some wise actions God will help us learn?** (How to show His love to others. How to be a good friend.) Pray, praising God for His gift of wisdom and asking for His help to live in wise ways.

Discussion Questions

1. What are some times kids your age need to be wise? (When tempted to do something wrong. When making a choice about how to treat others.)

2. The Bible tells us that God gives us wisdom. How can we get wisdom from God? (Ask God to help us make wise decisions, and then trust Him to answer our prayers. Think about what God's Word says to do and how to obey it.)

3. What does the Bible say are some wise ways to live? (Love others. Be kind. Tell the truth. Be generous to others.) **Why is it wise to live those ways?**

Additional Information for Older Children

King Solomon was known throughout the world for his wisdom. He wrote several books in the Bible, including Ecclesiastes. Ecclesiastes 3:1-13 is a list of different things that may happen to people. These verses are sometimes read at New Year's services. A volunteer reads Ecclesiastes 3:1-13 aloud.

Hidden Picture

We can worship Jesus as the Savior whom God sent for everyone in the world.

Scripture Background

Matthew 2:1-12

Teacher Materials

Bible with bookmark at John 8:12, a large picture (picture of wise men, nature scene, children or family scene, etc.), large Post-it Notes.

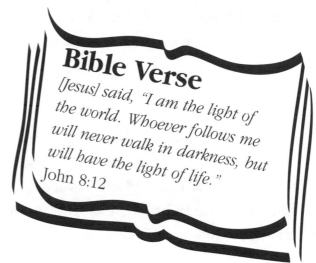

Bible Verse

[Jesus] said, "I am the light of the world. Whoever follows me will never walk in darkness, but will have the light of life."

John 8:12

Prepare the Activity

Completely cover large picture with rows of Post-it Notes.

Introduce the Object Talk

One of the best reasons to worship Jesus is because He is the Savior God sent for all the people of the world. In the Bible we read of some ways that people found out about this good news. Let's find out who these people were and how they learned and celebrated the fact that Jesus is the Savior for everyone!

Present the Object Talk

1. Display picture covered with Post-it Notes. **What picture might be hidden behind these Post-it Notes?** Invite one volunteer at a time to remove a Post-it Note, asking each to guess what the picture is. Continue until all Post-it Notes are removed.

2. It's always exciting to discover something that has been hidden. A long time ago in Bible times, some men traveled a long way to discover a new King. Who were these men and

who did they find? (The wise men who found and worshiped Jesus.) **The wise men were glad to have the Savior of the world shown to them when they came to Bethlehem. This discovery of the wise men is celebrated around the world at a special holiday on January 6 called Epiphany. Epiphany comes from a Greek word that means to show or reveal.**

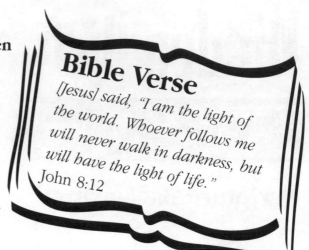

Bible Verse

[Jesus] said, "I am the light of the world. Whoever follows me will never walk in darkness, but will have the light of life."
John 8:12

Conclude

Removing the papers helped you reveal and see what the picture was. The wise men helped show everyone in the whole world that Jesus is God's Son and that He came to be the Savior of everyone in the world! Read John 8:12. When Jesus said He is the light of the world, He meant that He shows people of all countries how to know God. Pray, thanking Jesus for being the Savior of the world.

Discussion Questions

1. **What does it mean to worship Jesus?** (To show how much we love Him. To thank and praise Him.)

2. **What can we thank Jesus for doing?** (Loving us. Hearing and answering our prayers.)

3. **What are some other gifts we can give Jesus?** (Bring offering to church. Obey Jesus and show His love by caring for others. Thank Jesus when we pray.)

Additional Information for Older Children

The Bible tells us the wise men came from the East. (See Matthew 2:1.) **Many Bible students believe they came from the area around Babylon. The Jewish people had lived as captives for 70 years in Babylon. One of these captives was Daniel, the Old Testament prophet. The wise men may have learned about the promise of the Messiah from the writings of Daniel. Read some of Daniel's writings about the Messiah in Daniel 7:13,14.** Invite children to find and read these verses.

Washed Clean

Because God announced that Jesus is His Son, we can celebrate who Jesus is and become part of God's family.

Celebration

Baptism of Jesus Sunday

Scripture Background

Matthew 3:13-17

Teacher Materials

Bible with bookmark at 1 John 5:20, objects used for baptism in your church; optional—dirty drinking glass, bowl of soapy water, towel.

Bible Verse
The Son of God has come and has given us understanding, so that we may know him who is true. 1 John 5:20

Introduce the Object Talk

God announced that Jesus is His Son. When we believe that Jesus is God's Son, we show that we want to love and obey God with our actions. Let's look at some objects that remind us of one way of showing what we believe about Jesus.

Present the Object Talk

1. Display objects you brought that are used in your church for baptism. If children are familiar with objects, invite volunteers to tell about them. Explain how each object is used and the baptismal method your church uses. (Optional: Explain baptism in the following way: Show dirty glass. **Would you want to drink from this glass?** Wash glass and offer volunteer a drink. **We use water for cleaning. The Bible often compares washing with water to how God cleans the sin from our lives. Baptism is a special way to show that God washes us clean**

from sin and makes us ready to love and obey Him.) You may wish to invite your pastor or another church leader to come and explain the baptismal method used by your church.

2. Jesus was baptized when He lived on earth to show that He was ready to completely obey God. (Optional: Ask a volunteer to read Matthew 3:13-17 aloud.)

What are some ways we show love for God and obey Him? (Treat others in ways that please God. Tell others about Jesus.)

Bible Verse

The Son of God has come and has given us understanding, so that we may know him who is true. 1 John 5:20

Conclude

When Jesus was baptized, God was pleased and told the whole world that Jesus was His Son. When we are baptized, we are telling the world that we believe in Jesus as our Savior. Read 1 John 5:20 aloud. **This verse tells us that we can get to know who Jesus is. What are some ways we can get to know Jesus?** (Learn about Jesus at church. Study God's Word. Pray to Jesus.) Pray, asking for God's help to know more about Jesus.

Discussion Questions

1. **God spoke from heaven to tell everyone that Jesus is His Son. What are some ways people make announcements today?** (By e-mail or on a web page. Sending a letter or flyer. Telling the news on the radio or TV.)

2. **What did Jesus do as God's Son?** (Died to save all people from their sins. Healed people. Cared for the sick and the poor. Taught people how to love others.)

3. **How can we help people today learn that Jesus is God's Son?** (Invite them to church. Tell them stories about Jesus.)

Additional Information for Older Children

The Old Testament contains many prophecies about Jesus. The Old Testament prophet Isaiah wrote some words that describe the Savior God promised to send the world. Ask older children to find, read and compare Isaiah 42:1 and Matthew 3:17. **The words God spoke at Jesus' baptism let everyone know that Jesus was the Savior written about in the Old Testament.**

Bibles and Books

Scripture Background

Psalm 32

Teacher Materials

Bible with bookmark at Psalm 32:8, examples of instruction books (computer book, cookbook, appliance manual, textbook, etiquette book, etc.), one sheet of paper for each child.

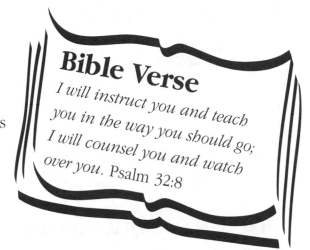

Bible Verse
I will instruct you and teach you in the way you should go; I will counsel you and watch over you. Psalm 32:8

Introduce the Object Talk

The Bible is a collection of books that tells us the good news about Jesus and helps us grow in God's family. Let's compare God's Word with other books that help us.

Present the Object Talk

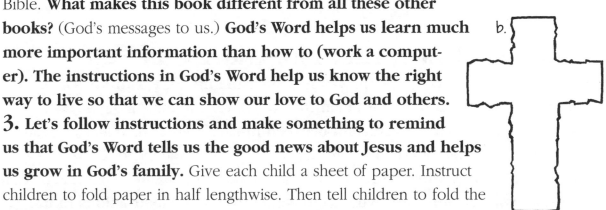

a.

1. Display examples of instruction books one at a time, and ask questions such as, **What kind of book is this? What does it help us do?** Volunteers respond. **What do all of these books have in common?** (Help people learn to do something.)
2. All of these books help us learn how to do things. Show Bible. **What makes this book different from all these other books?** (God's messages to us.) **God's Word helps us learn much more important information than how to (work a computer). The instructions in God's Word help us know the right way to live so that we can show our love to God and others.**
3. Let's follow instructions and make something to remind us that God's Word tells us the good news about Jesus and helps us grow in God's family. Give each child a sheet of paper. Instruct children to fold paper in half lengthwise. Then tell children to fold the

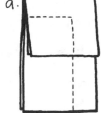

b.

top third down. Children tear out a rectangular shape from the nonfolded edges (see sketch a). When unfolded, children will have made a torn-paper cross (see sketch b). **When we see a cross, it reminds us of the way in which Jesus died to take the punishment for our sins. Jesus' death and resurrection are the good news the Bible tells us about.**

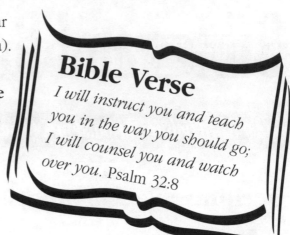

Bible Verse

I will instruct you and teach you in the way you should go; I will counsel you and watch over you. Psalm 32:8

Conclude

Read Psalm 32:8 aloud. **What does Psalm 32:8 say God will do for us?** (Instruct and teach us about the right way to live.) **What are some ways God teaches us?** (Through His Word. Through parents and teachers.) **God's instructions show us how to grow as members of God's family. This is a great reason to celebrate!** Pray, praising God and thanking Him for His help in learning the right way to live.

Discussion Questions

1. **What good news do you learn about Jesus from reading the Bible?** (Jesus died on the cross to pay for our sins. He rose from the dead. Jesus healed and cared for many people.)

2. **How does the Bible help us grow in God's family?** (The Bible tells us how to become a part of God's family: believe that Jesus died for our sins and ask for forgiveness. When we read the Bible, we can learn the good things God wants His family members to do.)

3. **When can you read or hear about God's Word?** (At school. Playing a game during recess. At home with family.)

4. **What are some of the ways the Bible tells us to live?** (Love God. Love our neighbors. Be kind and help others. Tell the truth. Obey our parents. Tell about God.)

Additional Information for Older Children

In some Bibles, two phrases are written under the title of Psalm 32: "Of David" and "A maskil." What does "of David" mean? (David wrote the psalm.) **David wrote this psalm as a conversation between himself and God.** Volunteers read verse 5 as an example of David's words and verse 8 as an example of God's Words. *Maskil* **is a Hebrew word which means "any who understand." That means that the psalm was written for anyone who would follow the instructions in it.**

Games to Go

Scripture Background

Psalm 121

Teacher Materials

Bible with bookmarks at Psalm 121 and Jeremiah 17:7, example(s) of travel games (travel-size board games, magnetic checker and chess sets, etc.).

Bible Verse

Blessed is the man who trusts in the Lord, whose confidence is in him. Jeremiah 17:7

Introduce the Object Talk

Wherever we go, we can trust God's promises to guide and protect us. Let's talk about some things we often do when we travel and discover how God's promises can help us all the time, not just when we travel.

Present the Object Talk

1. Show example(s) of travel games. **When might you play a game like this?** Volunteers respond. **What games do you play on trips with your family?** (Twenty Questions, the Alphabet Game, etc.) **What songs might you sing when you travel?** ("Bingo," "Old MacDonald," etc.) (Optional: Sing songs or play games children suggest.)

2. In Old Testament times, the people sang songs when they traveled, just like we do. Many of these songs are written for us in the book of Psalms. Ask a volunteer to read the first phrase written under Psalm 121: "A song of ascents." **The word "ascent" means to go or move upwards. This phrase means that the psalm was sung during a yearly trip, called a pilgrimage, to Jerusalem. Jerusalem and the Temple were located higher up on a mountain than most of the other towns in Israel, so the people would travel up**

to Jerusalem in order to worship God in the Temple. As they traveled, there must have been times when God's people were scared or worried. Singing this song reminded them of God's promises to love, guide and protect them. Read, or ask an older child to read, Psalm 121.

Bible Verse
Blessed is the man who trusts in the Lord, whose confidence is in him. Jeremiah 17:7

Conclude

Wherever we go, we can remember God's promises to guide and protect us, too. Read Jeremiah 17:7 aloud. **Who does this verse tell us is blessed?** (Anyone who trusts God.) **Who can give us confidence?** (The Lord.) Pray, praising God for His guidance and protection and thanking Him that we can trust in Him to keep us safe wherever we go.

Discussion Questions

1. **How do your parents or teachers give you guidance or instruction?** (Tell what to do. Write lists. Show how to do things.)

2. **When are some times kids your age need to pray and trust God for His guidance and protection?** (When there are hard jobs to do at home or at school. When others do mean things.)

3. **In what ways does God guide us?** (By His instructions in the Bible. By giving us people who tell us the right ways to love God and others. By answering our prayers.)

4. **What are some ways to show we trust God to be our guide?** (Ask His help when making choices. Read God's Word to discover His commands.)

Additional Information for Older Children

Just as we have different songs for different holidays and other occasions, people in Old Testament times had many different kinds of songs. The word "psalms" means "praises." The book of Psalms is actually 150 songs. Many of them are songs of praise to God. Psalms 120—134 are all Psalms of Ascent and are also known as the pilgrimage psalms because people sang them while going from one place to another.

Direction Signals

Loving and obeying God your whole life are the wisest things to do.

Scripture Background
Psalm 62

Teacher Materials
Bible with bookmarks at Psalm 62 and Mark 12:30, music cassette/CD or video and player.

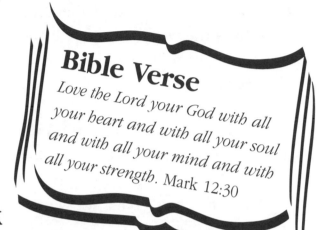

Bible Verse
Love the Lord your God with all your heart and with all your soul and with all your mind and with all your strength. Mark 12:30

Introduce the Object Talk
Loving God and obeying His directions our whole lives are the wisest things to do. Let's look at some ways people are directed to do things.

Present the Object Talk
1. Ask children to identify various hand directions or signals. For instance, place index finger in front of puckered lips. **What am I directing you to do when I do this?** (Be quiet.) Continue with hand directions that mean "come here," "go away," "stop," "time out" and so on. (Variation: Ask volunteers to suggest and demonstrate hand directions.)

2. Another time when hand directions are used is when a director is leading a band or a choir. Ask a volunteer to read the phrases written under Psalm 62: "For the director of music. For Jeduthun. A psalm of David." **Who wrote the psalm?** (David.) **Who is Jeduthun?** (The director of music.) **This psalm was written for the director of music, Jeduthun, to use when he directed the songs of praise to God during worship services.**

3. Lead children in singing a song from the music cassette/CD or video. Divide children into two groups. Ask a volunteer to alternately point to each group. Only group being pointed at sings. Volunteer may also use hand signals to direct each group in singing loudly or softly.

Conclude

Read Mark 12:30 aloud. **What are the four ways we are directed to love God?** Volunteers respond. **The more we love God, the more we want to obey Him. And that's the wisest thing we can do!** Pray, asking God for His help to love Him and obey His directions every day.

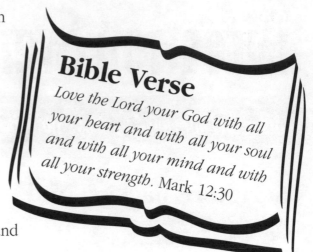

Bible Verse

Love the Lord your God with all your heart and with all your soul and with all your mind and with all your strength. Mark 12:30

Discussion Questions

1. **Why are loving and obeying God our whole lives the wisest things we can do?** (God tells us the best ways to live. We avoid making mistakes when we do things the way God tells us to.)

2. **Who are some Bible people who showed by their actions that they loved and obeyed God? What are some of those actions?**

3. **What can you do to show that you love and obey God?** (Praise Him with songs. Pray to God, telling God why you love Him. Obey God's commands in the Bible. Tell the truth. Care for others.)

Additional Information for Older Children

The Hebrew word *selah* **(SEE-lah) occurs twice in Psalm 62 as well as in many other psalms. No one really knows what** *selah* **means! Some people believe it is a musical direction that tells when the musicians should play loudly in between the phrases of the song. Other people think** *selah* **indicates when a pause in the singing should take place. Read Psalm 4 where the word** *selah* **appears and decide which definition you think is correct.** Guide children to find and read verses, and then discuss the usage of the word *selah.*

Gifts of Love

Celebration

Valentine's Day

Scripture Background

John 15:13

Teacher Materials

Bible with bookmarks at John 15:13 and
1 Corinthians 13:4, 8½ x11-inch (21.5x27.5-cm)
sheet of paper, scissors, marker, variety of Valentine's Day gifts
(heart-shaped candy box, valentine cards, flowers, etc.) in a large bag.

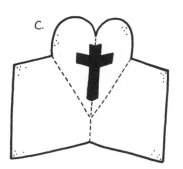

Bible Verse
Love is patient, love is kind.
1 Corinthians 13:4

Prepare the Activity

Make pop-up card. Fold and cut paper (see sketch a). Keeping card closed, fold as
shown in sketch b. Open the
card, draw and cut heart and
draw a cross (see sketch c).
Fold top portion of heart down
inside the card at an angle.
Decorate the front of the card
to resemble a valentine.

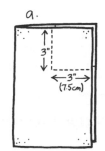
a.
3"
←3"→
(7.5cm)

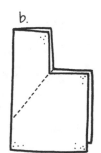
b.

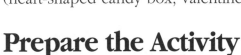
c.

Introduce the Object Talk

**The greatest love in all the world is God's love for us! Valentine's Day is a day
to thank God for His love and show love to others. Let's look at some of the
ways people tell others they are loved.**

Present the Object Talk

1. What kinds of things do people give each other on Valentine's Day? As children suggest gifts, display examples from the Valentine's Day gifts you brought.

2. On Valentine's Day we give cards and gifts to tell people that we love them. But the best, the greatest, gift of love ever given was not given on Valentine's Day. Open pop-up card you prepared. **What gift does this card remind you of?** (God's gift of salvation through His Son, Jesus.) **When was it given?** Volunteers respond. **God's gift of His Son, Jesus, is the greatest gift of love ever given.** Read, or ask an older child to read, John 15:13 aloud.

Bible Verse

Love is patient, love is kind.
1 Corinthians 13:4

Conclude

Listen to this verse which tells what we can do to show God's love to others. Read 1 Corinthians 13:4. **What are the ways to show love this verse tells us about?** (Be patient. Be kind.) **What are some ways you can show patience and kindness this week?** (Wait for someone else to share. Help someone who is hurt.) Pray, thanking God for His great love and His greatest gift, Jesus.

Discussion Questions

1. Why is God's love the greatest love of all? (He always loves us, no matter what. He is always patient and kind toward us. We may forget to love people all the time, but God always loves us.)

2. How does God show His love for us? (Sent Jesus to teach people about God and to die on the cross for our sins. Cared for people since the world began. Hears and answers our prayers. Gives us families and friends to love us.)

3. What words would you use to describe God's love to someone else? (Huge. The greatest. Faithful. Patient. Kind.)

4. What are some ways we can show God's love to others?

Additional Information for Older Children

There are several stories about who Saint Valentine was. According to tradition, around 270 a man named Valentine was put in prison because he worshiped God. While in prison, he continued to show love for God by helping others. Because of his faith, Valentine was killed. After his death, leaders in the church began a feast, or holiday, to help members of God's family remember His love.

Feelings Masks

Celebration

Ash Wednesday, Lent

Scripture Background

Psalm 51:10

Teacher Materials

Bible with bookmarks at Psalm 51:10 and 1 Corinthians 13:7, six large paper plates, marker; optional—paper plates, markers.

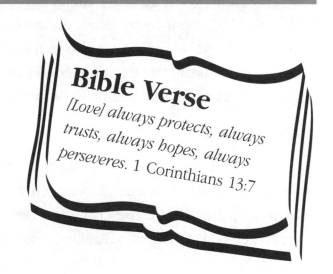

Bible Verse

[Love] always protects, always trusts, always hopes, always perseveres. 1 Corinthians 13:7

Prepare the Object Talk

Prepare paper plate masks as shown in sketch.

Introduce the Object Talk

God will always forgive us for the wrong things we do, if we feel truly sorry and ask for His forgiveness. Let's look at some ways people show how they are feeling.

Present the Object Talk

1. One at a time, ask volunteers to hold over their faces the masks you prepared. As each mask is shown, ask children to describe how the person might be feeling. Children imitate the expressions. (Optional: Children make their own masks.)

2. Show the mask with sad expression. **During the 40 days before Easter, many Christians think about the sad or wrong things they have done and ask God to**

help them love and obey Him. This time of year is called Lent. Ask a volunteer to read Psalm 51:10 as an example of a prayer people often pray during Lent. **On the first day of Lent, called Ash Wednesday, some people have a cross drawn with ashes on their foreheads. This cross shows that they**

believe and remember that Jesus died on a cross so that their sins can be forgiven.

Also during Lent, some people choose to give up eating favorite foods or doing certain things they like. Giving up things they like reminds them of how Jesus had to give up His life to show His love for them.
3. Thinking about Jesus' death on the cross does make us feel sad, but it also helps us get ready to celebrate the exciting, good news of Easter Sunday when Jesus was alive again. Show face with happy and/or excited expression.

Bible Verse

[Love] always protects, always trusts, always hopes, always perseveres. 1 Corinthians 13:7

Conclude

Read 1 Corinthians 13:7 aloud. **The word "persevere" means to keep doing something that is hard. It must have been very hard for Jesus to keep loving us and to give up His life on the cross, but He was willing to die so that we can have forgiveness of sins.** Pray, thanking God that He always forgives us when we're sorry for our sin.

Discussion Questions

1. **When might kids your age want to ask God's forgiveness?** (When they've been unkind to others. When they've told lies.)

2. **When is a good time to ask God to forgive us?** (Whenever we realize we have sinned, are sorry for the wrong things we have done and want to start doing right things.)

3. **How do we know that God will forgive us?** (God always keeps His promises. Jesus died on the cross to pay for our sins.)

4. **What are some ways to celebrate God's forgiveness of our sins?** (Sing songs to thank Him. Thank Him in our prayers. Forgive others. Tell others about God's forgiveness.)

Additional Information for Older Children

During Bible times, people wore an itchy shirt, called sackcloth, and covered themselves with dust or ashes to show that they were sorry for the wrong things they'd done. Read Jonah 3:4-10 to learn how the people of Nineveh not only gave up eating food but also wore sackcloth and ashes to show God they were sorry for their sin.

Memory Lane

Scripture Background

Psalm 105

Teacher Materials

Bible with bookmark at Psalm 105, baby book or photo album of baby pictures; optional—paper, pencils, markers.

Bible Verse

Sing to him, sing praise to him; tell of all his wonderful acts.
Psalm 105:2

Introduce the Object Talk

God shows His love for us through His actions. Often, we make memory books or photo albums showing the actions of other people. Let's look at an example of a memory book and find out how we can remember God's loving actions.

Present the Object Talk

1. How many of you know the name of the city where you were born? how old you were when you first walked? the day your first tooth came in?

Volunteers respond. Display baby book or photo album. **This is a special book that some parents put together to help them remember the actions of their children when they were babies.** Describe some of the contents of the baby book or photo album you brought.

2. In Old Testament times, God's people wanted to remember the loving actions of God. So when the people gathered together to celebrate special occasions, one of the priests would read special songs to remind the people of all the amazing things God had done for them. Read, or ask an older child to read, Psalm 105:1-5. **Psalm 105 describes some**

of the wonderful things God did for Abraham, Jacob, Joseph, Moses and all the Israelites! These reminders of God's loving care gave the Israelites good reason to celebrate! (Optional: Children write or draw their own reminders of things God has done for them and their families.)

Bible Verse

Sing to him, sing praise to him; tell of all his wonderful acts. Psalm 105:2

Conclude

Read Psalm 105:2 aloud. **What are some of the things God has done for you or your family?** Volunteers respond. **As we remember all the good things God has done for us, we have reason to celebrate, too!** Pray, thanking God for His love and all the great things He has done for us, remembering things mentioned by volunteers.

Discussion Questions

1. **When is a time a kid your age might experience God's loving care?** (When He answers prayer. When He provides food.)

2. **What are some good ways to learn more about God's loving acts?** (Read the Bible. Ask older people who love God about His great acts.)

3. **What has God done for you or people you know to show His love?** (Given families to care for us. Given us a house to be warm in. Given us people to tell about Him.)

4. **What can you do to tell others about God's loving acts?**

Additional Information for Older Children

Many psalms were written by David to praise God. Often we can find out what was happening in David's life at the time he wrote a particular psalm. Find Psalm 105:1-15 and 1 Chronicles 16:8-22 in your Bibles. Compare the verses in these passages. Children read verses and describe similarities and differences. Then ask children to read 1 Chronicles 16:1 to find the event for which David wrote these words.

Honorable Mention

Celebration
Blessing of the Children

Scripture Background
Matthew 19:13-15; Mark 10:13-16; Luke 18:15-17

Teacher Materials
Bible with bookmarks at Matthew 19:14,15; and
1 John 3:1; objects used to recognize deserving
people (trophy, blue ribbon, certificate, award, etc.).

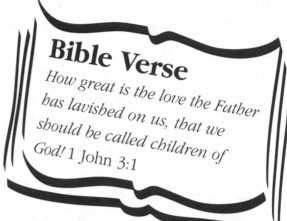

Bible Verse
How great is the love the Father has lavished on us, that we should be called children of God! 1 John 3:1

Prepare the Activity
Place objects around room. (Optional: Arrange to have a pastor or other church
leader say a prayer of blessing for the children.)

Introduce the Object Talk
**Each of you is important to God! Let's talk about some of the ways we show we
think people are important.**

Present the Object Talk
1. What are some awards or honors you've received? contests you've won?
Volunteers respond. **When people win contests or are given awards, we find
ways to let them know what they
did was important.** Ask volunteers to
search for and identify the objects you
placed around the room.
**2. Many times today people are
honored because they have done
something special. But Jesus didn't
honor children because they had**

done something special. Jesus loves all children. Jesus made sure the disciples knew children were important to Him when He showed how glad He was to see them. Read Matthew 19:14,15. **Jesus recognized how important children are. Today many countries, schools and other organizations set aside special days on which to honor children and show how important they are.**

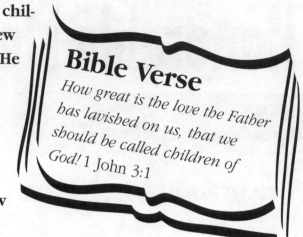

Bible Verse

How great is the love the Father has lavished on us, that we should be called children of God! 1 John 3:1

3. **Some churches have a Sunday on which children are honored. On this day, a special prayer or blessing is said for each child. When we bless someone, it means we ask God to do good things for the person.**
(Optional: Pastor or other church leader says a blessing for the children.)

Conclude

Read 1 John 3:1 aloud. **When we are members of God's family, we know that we are loved by God and important to Him.** Pray, thanking God for His love and asking Him to show His care and protection to each child in the group.

Discussion Questions

1. **How are important people usually treated?** (Given a red carpet. Given a special seat. Get driven around in a special car. Have people to help them do everything.)

2. **How do we know that we are important to God?** (The Bible tells us. We are called His children.)

3. **What things does God do to show you that you are important to Him?** (Listens to an answers my prayers. Sent Jesus to take the punishment for my sins so that I can live forever with God. Gives me people who love and care for me.)

Additional Information for Older Children

Many countries, including Japan, Australia and Turkey, have national holidays in honor of children. In Turkey on Children's Day, children switch places with government leaders. The president, prime minister, the cabinet minister, and city and state leaders turn over their jobs to children who even sign laws into effect!

Thundering Sounds

Because God's power is greater than anything, He can help us when we're afraid.

Scripture Background
Psalm 29

Teacher Materials
Bible with bookmarks at Psalm 29 and John 14:27; optional—picture of a storm, objects to make sound effects for rain and thunder (cookie sheet, drum, rain stick).

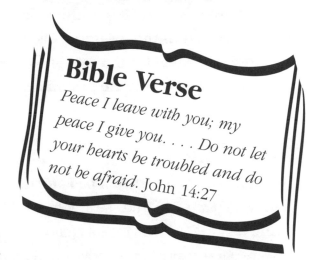

Bible Verse
Peace I leave with you; my peace I give you. . . . Do not let your hearts be troubled and do not be afraid. John 14:27

Introduce the Object Talk
When we're afraid, God can help us because His power is the greatest thing there is. Let's look at some of the ways we can see God's power in nature.

Present the Object Talk
1. What kinds of sounds do you hear during a thunderstorm? How do you think we could make the sounds of a thunderstorm? Volunteers respond.
(Optional: Display picture of a storm.)

2. Children suggest and practice three sounds which can be used to represent a thunderstorm (rubbing palms together, snapping fingers, patting legs, stomping feet, etc.).

After practicing sounds, divide children into three groups and assign an order in which to make sounds. (Optional: Ask an older child to lead each group.) Direct children to make sounds as in a round. The first group begins a sound, followed in five to eight seconds by the second group and then the third group. When the first group begins a different sound, the other groups

continue with the old sound until directed to change. (Optional: Children use objects to make sound effects for rain and thunder.)

3. The sound of thunder is one way the Bible describes God's power. Read or ask older children to read Psalm 29:3,4,7 aloud. **These verses help us discover what God's power is like. How is the voice of God described in this psalm?** (Majestic. Powerful. Like thunder and lightning.) **God's power is greater than anything He has made.**

Bible Verse

Peace I leave with you; my peace I give you. . . . Do not let your hearts be troubled and do not be afraid. John 14:27

Conclude

When have you been in a bad storm? How did you feel when you heard thunder? Volunteers respond. Read John 14:27 aloud. **What does this verse tell us about being afraid?** (When we feel afraid, God promises to help us feel peaceful.) Pray, praising God for His great power and thanking Him for His help when we're afraid.

Discussion Questions

1. What are some powerful things that kids your age might be afraid of? (Storms. Earthquakes. Tornadoes.)

2. Why can God help us when we are afraid of these things? (Because He is the one true God. God created everything. He is more powerful than anything He created. He loves us and wants to help us.)

3. How does God help us when we are afraid? (Answers our prayers. Gives us adults to help us feel safe. Helps us remember His power. Gives us courage and peace.)

Additional Information for Older Children

Psalm 29 is a psalm of praise to God. This psalm has been called "The Psalm of the Seven Thunders" because it refers to the voice of God seven times. Many books of the Bible show God's power by comparing His voice to thunder. Children read the following Scriptures that compare God's voice to thunder: Job 37:5; Psalm 68:32,33; Jeremiah 10:12,13.

Sending Portions

God's power helps us accomplish His plans.

Celebration
Purim

Scripture Background
Esther 9:18-32

Teacher Materials
Bible with bookmarks at Esther 9 and
Psalm 33:11, basket; optional—canned foods.

Bible Verse

The plans of the Lord stand firm forever, the purposes of his heart through all generations. Psalm 33:11

Introduce the Object Talk
God has many good things He wants us to do and with His power, He helps us to do them. Queen Esther, who lived long ago in Old Testament times, rescued her people to keep them safe as God had planned. Her brave and good actions are remembered with a special holiday called Purim (POO-rihm). Let's find out how this holiday is celebrated.

Present the Object Talk
1. Display the basket you brought. **If you were to fill this basket with food for a friend, what would you put in it?** Volunteers answer. Repeat with gifts for a neighbor, a teacher and a grandparent. (Optional: Put canned foods in basket to make a gift for a needy person.) **Giving gifts to others, especially those in need, is one of the ways Purim is celebrated.**

2. Purim is also celebrated by reading aloud the whole book of Esther. As the story is read, children in costumes act out the story of how God's people were saved. The audience cheers the good characters and boos the bad characters in the story. Purim is a day for celebrating God's power and doing

good things to help others. The custom of giving gifts to friends and to the poor is written about in the book of Esther. Read Esther 9:22 aloud. **This custom is called Shalach Manot (shah-LAHK muh-NOHT).** (In English *Shalach Manot* means "sending portions.")

Bible Verse
The plans of the Lord stand firm forever, the purposes of his heart through all generations. Psalm 33:11

Conclude

When we do things that show our love and obedience to God, we are following God's plans for us. Read Psalm 33:11 aloud. **This verse helps us learn that God's power is so strong that nothing can keep His plans from taking place. What are some of the good things God wants us to do?** (Receive His love. Become a member of God's family. Talk to God in prayer.) Pray, asking for God's help to do the good things He wants us to do.

Discussion Questions

1. **What did Esther and her people celebrate on Purim?** (Esther's brave actions. The defeat of Haman. God's power and care for them.)

2. **What are some of the good things God has helped you do?** (Be kind to a brother or sister. Tell others about Him. Help someone who was in danger.)

3. **What are some ways to learn more of the good things God has planned for you to do?** (Read God's commands in the Bible. Ask teachers or older Christians. Pray to God.)

Additional Information for Older Children

The word "Purim" is the plural form of a Hebrew word that means "lots." The name refers to the way in which the evil Haman decided which day to destroy the Jews. Haman cast lots, a phrase that means to choose something by chance—like drawing straws or participating in a lottery. Another way in which Purim is celebrated is by eating a special pastry called *hamantaschen*. This pastry is shaped like a triangle to remind people of the shape of Haman's hat.

Passover Power

Whenever we need help, we can depend on God's power.

Celebration

Feast of Unleavened Bread, Passover

Scripture Background

Exodus 12:1-27; Deuteronomy 16:1-8

Teacher Materials

Bible with bookmark at Exodus 12:24-27 and Psalm 46:1, bite-size pieces of unleavened bread (or *matzo* crackers) and bread prepared with yeast, two paper plates.

Prepare the Activity

Put each type of bread on a different plate.

Introduce the Object Talk

We can depend on God's power whenever we need help. Long ago in Old Testament times, God helped the Israelites escape from slavery in Egypt. Let's find out how God told His people to remember and celebrate His great power and help.

Present the Object Talk

1. As part of this celebration God told His people to eat a special kind of bread. Children eat samples of each type of bread. **What are the differences you can find by touching and tasting the two different kinds of bread?** Volunteers respond. Identify which is unleavened bread. **Because unleavened bread does not have yeast in it, it doesn't rise or puff up into a loaf shape when it is baked, and it can be made very quickly. Why do you think the Israelites only had time to make unleavened bread?** (They were in a hurry to escape from Egypt.)

2. What else do you remember about the Israelites' escape from Egypt? (God

> ## Bible Verse
> God is our refuge and strength, an ever-present help in trouble.
> Psalm 46:1

sent 10 plagues to convince Pharaoh, the Egyptian ruler, to let the people leave.) **The name of this holiday, Passover, comes from the last plague. God had given the Israelites special instructions to paint on their doorposts the blood of a lamb. On the night the Israelites escaped from Egypt, in any house that did not have the lamb's blood painted on its doorposts, the oldest son would die. Because death passed over the Israelite homes, the holiday is called Passover. The lamb killed at this celebration was called the Passover Lamb. Jesus is called our Passover Lamb because He gave His life to rescue us from sin.**

Bible Verse

God is our refuge and strength, an ever-present help in trouble. Psalm 46:1

3. **The Passover celebration helps people remember God's power.** Read, or ask an older child to read, Exodus 12:24-27.

Conclude

God's power helps us today, too. Read Psalm 46:1 aloud. **What do you learn about God from Psalm 46:1?** Pray, thanking God that we can depend on His power.

Discussion Questions

1. **When are some times kids your age need God's help?**

2. **When are some times God has helped you?** Tell your own answer before volunteers respond.

3. **What can we do to receive God's help?** (Pray to God and ask for His help. Read what God tells us to do in the Bible.)

4. **Why can we depend on God's power and help?** (He loves us. He keeps His promises.)

Additional Information for Older Children

Yeast spreads through dough and causes the bread to rise, or get bigger. How does yeast remind us of sin? (When a person sins, it can spread through his or her life.) **Throughout Scripture, yeast is compared to sin. Read 1 Corinthians 5:6-8 to find what the apostle Paul wrote about sin and how Jesus' death on the cross takes away our sin.**

Passover Plates

Celebration

Feast of Unleavened Bread, Passover

Scripture Background

Exodus 12:1-14

Teacher Materials

Bible with bookmarks at Exodus 12:14 and
Psalm 77:12,13; plate; several of these
foods—parsley, salt water, horseradish, *matzo* crack-
ers, *haroset* (chopped apples and nuts mixed with honey), lamb or other
clean bone, hard-boiled egg; optional—*seder* plate.

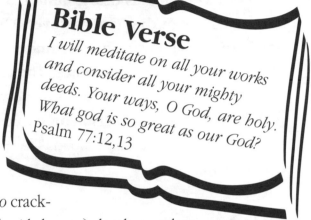

Bible Verse

*I will meditate on all your works
and consider all your mighty
deeds. Your ways, O God, are holy.
What god is so great as our God?*
Psalm 77:12,13

Introduce the Object Talk

It's important to praise God and remember all that He has done for us. After
God rescued His people from slavery in Egypt, He told them to eat a special
meal to help them remember and celebrate His help and protection. Let's find
out what foods are eaten at this special meal.

Present the Object Talk

**1. What is the name of the celebration at which God's rescue of His people
from slavery is remembered?** (Passover.) **Another name for
the Passover meal is *seder* (SAY-dehr). *Seder* means
"order." As the foods are eaten in order, questions are
asked and answered to tell the story of the escape
from Egypt.**
2. Show and discuss each food item you brought.
(Optional: Place food items on seder plate. Invite volunteers to taste items.) **The Hebrew word for green plants is
karpas (CAHR-pahs). This green parsley reminds us that
everything that grows is a gift from God.** Dip parsley in salt water. **The salt water**

reminds us of the tears of the Hebrew slaves in Egypt. Place horseradish on a piece of *matzo*. **The horseradish tastes bitter and reminds us of the terrible years of slavery in Egypt.** *Haroset,* **made with apples, nuts and honey, reminds us of the mortar between the bricks that the Hebrew slaves used to build in Egypt. The bone reminds us of the lamb that was sacrificed at the first Passover. The hard-boiled egg is another reminder of the sacrifices made by God's people in Bible times. The** *matzo* **crackers (***matzo* **is bread made quickly without yeast) remind us how fast the Hebrews left Egypt.**

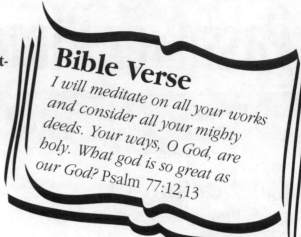

Bible Verse

I will meditate on all your works and consider all your mighty deeds. Your ways, O God, are holy. What god is so great as our God? Psalm 77:12,13

3. **Why did God want His people to celebrate the Passover?** Read, or ask an older child to read, Exodus 12:14 aloud. **The Passover celebration reminds us all of God's power.**

Conclude

Read Psalm 77:12,13 aloud. **What does Psalm 77:12,13 tell us about God?** (God is holy. He is the greatest.) Pray, asking for God's help to remember all the great things He has done and thanking Him for His love and power.

Discussion Questions

1. **What are some of the great things God has done that you have read about in the Bible?** (Helped the Israelites escape from Pharaoh's army. Helped the Hebrew people get to the Promised Land. Healed people. Sent Jesus to die for our sins.)

2. **What are some of the great things God has done for you and your family?** Tell your own answer as well as inviting volunteers to respond.

3. **When can you praise God for the ways He helps you?**

Additional Information for Older Children

During the *seder* **meal, a large cup is placed in the center of the table for the Old Testament prophet Elijah. In Old Testament times, people believed that Elijah would appear to announce the coming of the Messiah. Placing a cup on the table showed that the people were ready for the Messiah. Now we know that the Messiah, Jesus, has already come!**

Breaking Bread Together

Jesus' love for us is so great, He was willing to die on the cross.

Celebration

Communion, Maundy Thursday, Good Friday

Scripture Background

Matthew 26:17-30; Mark 14:12-26; Luke 22:7-20;
John 13:34,35

Bible Verse

This is how we know what love is: Jesus Christ laid down his life for us. 1 John 3:16

Teacher Materials

Bible with bookmarks at John 13:34,35 and
1 John 3:16; objects used by your church for communion (plates,
cups, chalice, bread or wafers, juice, etc.).

Introduce the Object Talk

**Because He loves us so much, Jesus was willing to die on the cross so that our
sins could be forgiven. The night before He was killed, Jesus ate a special supper with His disciples. Let's look at the way our church family remembers that
special supper and Jesus' death on the cross.**

Present the Object Talk

1. Show objects one at a time. **What is this object? What are some ways to use it?**
(Optional: Children taste food items.)

**2. We use these objects when we celebrate
the Lord's Supper. One of the names for
this celebration is "communion," which
means to share something with others.
When we celebrate communion together,
we share in celebrating and remembering
the last supper Jesus ate with His disciples**

before He died on the cross to take the punishment for our sins. Explain and
demonstrate use of objects. (Optional: Invite your pastor or other church leader to talk
with children about how your church celebrates the Lord's Supper.)

3. One special day each year, many Christians celebrate Jesus' last supper with His disciples; this day is called Maundy Thursday. The word "maundy" comes from the Latin word *mandatus* which means "command." Read, or ask an older child to read, John 13:34,35 aloud. **What is the new commandment Jesus gave His followers during the Last Supper?**

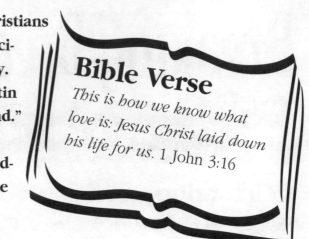

Bible Verse
This is how we know what love is: Jesus Christ laid down his life for us. 1 John 3:16

Conclude

Read 1 John 3:16 aloud. **What does this verse tell us that love really is?** (Jesus cares so much for us that He died for us.) Pray, thanking Jesus for dying on the cross for our sins. Talk with interested children about becoming members of God's family (see "Leading a Child to Christ" on pp. 16-17).

Discussion Questions

1. **What are some ways Jesus loved and served people when He was here on earth?** (Healed them. Fed them. Taught them the best way to live. Washed the disciples' feet.)

2. **How does Jesus show love for us today?** (Answers our prayers. Promises to always be with us.)

3. **What are some ways we can show Jesus' love to people today?** (Be patient with brothers or sisters. Help others at school. Play games fairly.)

Additional Information for Older Children

The day on which Jesus died is sometimes called Good Friday. No one knows for sure where the name Good Friday came from. Some people think that the word "good" came from the phrase "God's Friday." Other people, however, believe the name came about because even though Jesus' death was very sad, so much good happened as a result of His death. What are some of the good things that happened as a result of Jesus' death and resurrection? (Our sins can be forgiven. We can experience God's love.)

Welcoming Ways

Jesus is so great that we can't help but praise Him.

Celebration
Palm Sunday

Scripture Background
Matthew 21:1-17; Mark 11:1-11; Luke 19:28-40;
John 12:12-19

Teacher Materials
Bible with bookmark at Psalm 147:1; optional—
objects used to welcome and praise others (medal, red carpet,
confetti, pennants, pom poms, etc.).

Bible Verse
Praise the Lord. How good it is to sing praises to our God, how pleasant and fitting to praise him! Psalm 147:1

Introduce the Object Talk
We can't help but praise and honor Jesus because He is so great! Let's look at some of the ways great people are honored.

Present the Object Talk
1. One at a time, pantomime, or ask volunteers to pantomime, ways to praise or honor people. (Lay out a red carpet, drop flower petals down an aisle, cheer for a sports team, salute, bow, curtsy, throw confetti, etc.) As each action is pantomimed, children guess the action. **Who might be honored that way?** (Optional: Show objects used to honor others and ask children to describe how objects could be used to praise others.)

2. Why do we do special things to praise people? (To show they are important to us. To show that we admire or love them.) **On the first Palm Sunday, people praised and honored Jesus when He arrived in Jerusalem. They clapped and cheered, waved palm branches in the air and laid palm branches and their coats on the road for Jesus to ride on.**

Every year we remember and celebrate Palm Sunday because it was the beginning of the time when Jesus died for our sins and then rose again to give us new life.

Conclude

During the week that followed Jesus' kingly parade into Jerusalem, Jesus died on the cross to make a way for all of us to become members of God's family. He deserves all the honor we can give Him! Read Psalm 147:1 aloud. **What are some of the things God has done in your life for which you would like to praise and honor Him?** Praise God in prayer, mentioning children's responses.

Discussion Questions

1. **What are some of the reasons we want to praise Jesus?** (He is God's Son. He was willing to die on the cross to pay the punishment for all people's sins. He rose from the dead. He loves us all. He taught us the best way to live.)

2. **What are some ways we can praise Jesus?** (Sing songs to Him. When we pray, tell Him why we love Him or what we are thankful for. Tell others how wonderful He is.)

3. **What is your favorite way to praise Jesus?** Volunteers respond.

Additional Information for Older Children

We may not think of a donkey as a royal animal; but in Bible times, the donkey was considered a sign of humility, peace and royalty! Read 1 Kings 1:38-40 to learn about a kingly parade similar to the one we celebrate on Palm Sunday.

In Zechariah 9:9, you can read the Old Testament prophet Zechariah's prediction of a King coming to save God's people—riding on a donkey! Now we know the King he wrote about was Jesus! Volunteer reads verse aloud.

Great Greetings

Jesus' death and resurrection make it possible for us to have eternal life.

Celebration

Easter

Scripture Background

Matthew 26:36—28:15; Mark 14:32—16:8;
Luke 22:47—24:12; John 18—20:18

Teacher Materials

Bible with bookmark at 1 John 5:11, cassette/CD
or music video and player.

Bible Verse

God has given us eternal life,
and this life is in his Son.
1 John 5:11

Introduce the Object Talk

Because Jesus died for our sins and rose again, we can have eternal life! Let's look at one way we remember Jesus' great gift every year at Easter.

Present the Object Talk

1. Wave hand at children. **What does it mean when I wave my hand at you?** (Waving is a way to say hello or greet someone.) Demonstrate, or ask children to

demonstrate, other ways to greet people. (Say hello. Give a high five. Shake hands.)

2. During Easter, many Christians greet each other in a special way. One person says "Christ is risen," and the other says "He is risen indeed." For several minutes, play a song from the cassette/CD or music video as children walk around room and greet each other in the manner described above. (Note: If there are other Easter traditions followed in your church family, explain these traditions to children.)

Conclude

Jesus' resurrection makes it possible for us to become members of God's family! Read 1 John 5:11 aloud. **Eternal life means we can live with God in heaven, experiencing His love forever. According to this verse, where can we get eternal life?** (From God's Son, Jesus.) Pray, thanking Jesus for dying on the cross and rising from the dead so that we can have eternal life. Talk with interested children about becoming members of God's family (see "Leading a Child to Christ" on pp. 16-17).

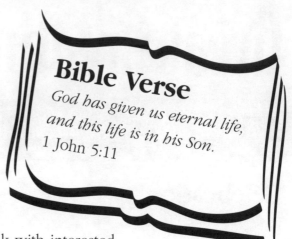

Bible Verse

God has given us eternal life, and this life is in his Son.
1 John 5:11

Discussion Questions

1. **Why was Jesus the only One who could take the punishment for our sins?** (Jesus is the only person who never sinned. He is the One God promised to send.)

2. **When we choose to become members of God's family, what does He give us?** (Forgiveness for our sins. Eternal life.)

3. **What are some ways we remember Jesus' death and celebrate His resurrection?** (Thank Jesus for His love. Sing special songs. Celebrate Easter with our church families at special worship services.)

4. **How does your family celebrate Jesus' resurrection at Eastertime?**

Additional Information for Older Children

Passion Week, also called Holy Week, begins with Palm Sunday and ends with Easter. Many churches are open for services daily or at least on Thursday and Friday as well as Sunday. This is the week during which Lent, which began 40 days earlier, ends. During Lent, many people choose to give up something they like or enjoy, in order to focus more on what Jesus gave up for them.

Believe It or Not

Believe that Jesus is alive, and accept His love for you!

Celebration

Easter

Scripture Background

John 20:19-31

Teacher Materials

Bible with bookmarks at John 3:16 and
John 20:29; objects for children to describe
(unusual stuffed animal, kitchen utensil, tool, etc.),
placed in a bag.

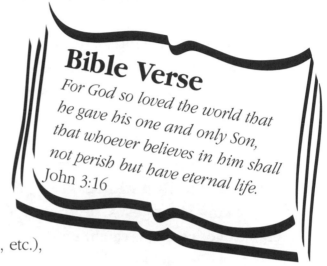

Bible Verse

For God so loved the world that he gave his one and only Son, that whoever believes in him shall not perish but have eternal life.
John 3:16

Introduce the Object Talk

We accept Jesus' love for us and believe that He is alive, even though we didn't see Him for ourselves! Let's try an experiment to discover why it sometimes might be hard to believe what other people tell us about something we didn't see for ourselves.

Present the Object Talk

1. Several volunteers leave the room (or close eyes). Show one of the objects and give children several moments to look at it. **When the volunteers return, describe the object to them, but don't use the words ("stuffed" or "animal").** Volunteers return and try to guess what the object is based on children's descriptions. Repeat for each object you brought, reminding children not to use obvious words that would give away the object's identity.

2. **What made it difficult to figure out what the object was?** Volunteers respond. **Sometimes it's hard to believe something is true if you haven't seen it yourself. When Jesus rose from the dead, Thomas, one of His disciples, didn't believe Jesus was really alive because he hadn't seen Jesus with his own eyes.**

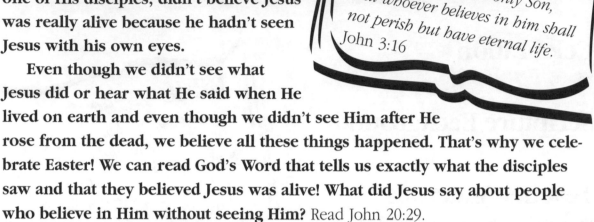

Bible Verse

For God so loved the world that he gave his one and only Son, that whoever believes in him shall not perish but have eternal life.
John 3:16

Even though we didn't see what Jesus did or hear what He said when He lived on earth and even though we didn't see Him after He rose from the dead, we believe all these things happened. That's why we celebrate Easter! We can read God's Word that tells us exactly what the disciples saw and that they believed Jesus was alive! What did Jesus say about people who believe in Him without seeing Him? Read John 20:29.

3. **Thinking about Jesus' death on the cross does make us feel sad, but it also helps us get ready to celebrate the exciting, good news of Easter Sunday when Jesus was alive again.** Ask children to demonstrate a face with happy and/or excited expression.

Conclude

Because we know Jesus is alive, we can also have eternal life—life that lasts forever with God in heaven. Read John 3:16 aloud. Pray, thanking God that Jesus is alive and that He loves us.

Discussion Questions

1. **What are some of the things you believe about Jesus?** (He loves me. He forgives the wrong things I do. He makes it possible for me to be part of God's family.)

2. **Who has helped you learn to believe in Jesus?** (Sunday School teacher. Parent.)

3. **In what ways do kids your age show they believe that Jesus is alive?** (Pray to Him. Obey His commands. Read the Bible to learn more about Him.)

Additional Information for Older Children

Jesus appeared several times to many different people in the days immediately following his resurrection. You can read about Jesus' appearance to two men traveling on the road to Emmaus in Luke 24:13-35.

Out of Sight

Jesus promises to care for the members of His family now and in the future.

Celebration

Ascension Sunday

Scripture Background

Matthew 28:16-20; Acts 1:1-11

Teacher Materials

Bible with bookmarks at John 14:3 and Acts 1:11.

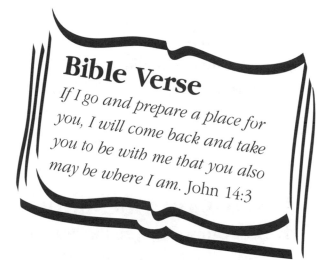

Bible Verse

If I go and prepare a place for you, I will come back and take you to be with me that you also may be where I am. John 14:3

Introduce the Object Talk

Both now and in the future, Jesus will care for the members of His family. He promised to always be with us. Jesus gave this promise when He lived on earth. Let's find out what happened.

Present the Object Talk

1. Take children outside (or ask several volunteers to stand near a window). **Look at something near your feet. What do you see?** Volunteers describe what they see. **Look at something a few feet away. What do you see?** Continue a few more times until children identify the farthest things they can see.

2. On the day when Jesus promised to be with us, His disciples looked as far up into the sky as they could see. Why were they looking up into the sky? (Jesus had left the earth to return to heaven.) **Jesus' return to heaven is sometimes called the ascension. The word "ascend" means to go up. The day of Jesus' return to heaven and the promise He made just before He left is so important**

that many Christians celebrate this special day every year. On this day, called Ascension Sunday, we remember that Jesus went up to heaven where He rules the whole world. We also remember that He's coming back again some day! Read, or ask an older child to read, Acts 1:11.

Bible Verse

If I go and prepare a place for you, I will come back and take you to be with me that you also may be where I am. John 14:3

Conclude

Jesus promised to take care of the members of His family for all time. Read John 14:3 aloud. **What does this verse tell us Jesus is doing to care for us in heaven?** (He's preparing a place for us so that we can be with Him forever.) Pray, thanking God for His loving care and that we can always depend on Him to care for us.

Discussion Questions

1. **How can we be sure that Jesus will keep His promise to care for us?** (Jesus always keeps His promises. He's cared for us and others in the past. The Bible tells us about Jesus' care for us.)

2. **What does Jesus do to care for us?** (Answers our prayers. Forgives our sins. Helps us obey Him.)

3. **When do you or someone in your family need to remember that Jesus is always with you?** (When we need courage to do what's right. When we need help in stopping an argument with friends. When we want to tell others about Jesus.)

Additional Information for Older Children

Before He died on the cross, Jesus told His disciples that even though He was going away, He would not leave them alone. His ascension did not mean that He was leaving His friends but that He would be with them in a whole new way. Read in John 14:15-21 about Jesus' promise to ask God to send the Holy Spirit to be with His believers.

Gifts to Honor

God gives us people to guide and care for us.

Celebration

Mother's Day

Scripture Background

Exodus 20:12

Teacher Materials

Bible with bookmarks at Exodus 20:12 and Proverbs 3:5,6; several gifts traditionally given on Mother's Day (candy, flowers, cards, etc.).

Bible Verse

Trust in the Lord with all your heart and lean not on your own understanding; in all your ways acknowledge him, and he will make your paths straight. Proverbs 3:5,6

Introduce the Object Talk

One of the ways God cares for us is by giving us people to guide and care for us. Let's look at ways we can honor these people who are gifts from God.

Present the Object Talk

1. One at a time, display the gifts you brought. **Who might you give this gift to? Why would you give this gift?** Repeat for each of the gifts you brought.

2. On Mother's Day, we give gifts like these to mothers and other people who care for us. Read Exodus 20:12 aloud. **Giving gifts is one way to honor people who care for us and let them know we appreciate all that they do for us. There are lots of types of mothers—grandmothers, stepmothers, foster mothers and**

people who act like mothers! They are all given to us by God to guide and care for us. **Who are some other people God has given to care for you?** (Fathers. Aunts. Older brothers or sisters. Teachers.) Invite volunteers to tell ways people care for them.

3. This year on Mother's Day, you can honor your mother or anyone else who guides you and cares for you. **What are some special or unusual ways to honor this person?** (Say, "I love you." Give a back massage. Water flowers. Clean your room and bathroom. Cook dinner.)

Bible Verse

Trust in the Lord with all your heart and lean not on your own understanding; in all your ways acknowledge him, and he will make your paths straight. Proverbs 3:5,6

Conclude

Read Proverbs 3:5,6 aloud. **According to these verses, whose directions should we follow?** (God's directions.) **How can we know what God wants us to do?** (By reading God's Word. By listening to parents and other people who guide and care for us.) Pray, thanking God that He gives us people to guide and care for us.

Discussion Questions

1. Who are the people you want to honor today? How do they guide and care for you?

2. What are some ways we need to be cared for? What are some good reasons to have people to guide us? (To help us know what to do in our lives. To teach us good ways to live.)

3. Who are some people who teach you about God? What can you do to thank God for giving you people to guide you in knowing Him?

Additional Information for Older Children

Mother's Day in the United States was first suggested by Julia Ward Howe (who wrote the words to the "Battle Hymn of the Republic") in 1872; the holiday was first celebrated nationally in 1914. Other countries around the world (such as France and Yugoslavia) have also established spring days to honor mothers. England observes Mothering Sunday, a custom dating back to the Middle Ages when worshipers returned to their "mother" churches for special services.

Weeks of Celebration

Celebration

Feast of Weeks, Firstfruits, Shavuot

Scripture Background

Leviticus 23:15-21

Teacher Materials

Bible with bookmarks at Leviticus 23:17 and
Psalm 119:66, two loaves of bread, honey,
softened cream cheese (8 oz.), small bowl, plastic knives, napkins.

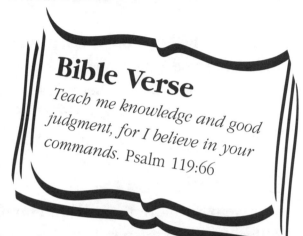

Bible Verse
Teach me knowledge and good judgment, for I believe in your commands. Psalm 119:66

Introduce the Object Talk

We can learn the best way to live by studying God's Word. People in the Old Testament celebrated a holiday which reminded them of the time when God gave His Law to Moses. They called this holiday the Feast of Weeks. Let's find out how the holiday was named and what the people did to celebrate it.

Present the Object Talk

1. The Feast of Weeks is celebrated seven weeks plus one day after the Passover celebration. Another name for this holiday is Shavuot (shah-voo-OHT) which is the Hebrew word for "weeks."

2. At this celebration, God told His people that two loaves of bread were to be waved as an offering, or gift, to God. Wave loaves of bread in the air as a demonstration. Read, or ask an older child to read, Leviticus 23:17. **At this time of the year, the harvest of grains used to make bread had just been completed, and the people were glad to thank God for the food they would make from the grains.**

3. Today the two loaves of bread remind us of the two tablets on which God wrote the Ten Commandments He gave to Moses. God gave the Ten Commandments so that His people would have His Word to help them. During the Feast of Weeks, Jewish people read the Ten Commandments aloud.

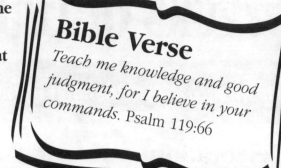

Bible Verse
Teach me knowledge and good judgment, for I believe in your commands. Psalm 119:66

4. During the Feast of Weeks, it is also traditional to eat dairy products as reminders of God's Word, which is "sweet" because it gives us what we need to grow in our knowledge of God. Mix small amounts of honey with cream cheese to form a spread. Spread mixture on bread. Cut bread into quarters and serve.

Conclude

Now we have more than the Ten Commandments to help us learn the best way to live. We have the whole Bible to help us! Read Psalm 119:66 aloud. **To have good judgment means to be wise and know the right things to do and say. We know that we can depend on God to help us be wise and make good choices.** Pray, asking God's help in doing what's right.

Discussion Questions

1. What are some of the commands God gives us in the Bible? (Love God more than anything. Love your neighbor. Forgive each other. Do not lie. Do not steal. Honor your parents. Treat others fairly. Say kind words.)

2. What is one way you can follow these commands this week? Volunteers respond.

3. When you need help following God's commands, what can you do? (Ask God for help to obey. Talk to your mom or dad about what to do.)

Additional Information for Older Children

The Bible uses word pictures to describe God's Word and the ways in which it helps us. Children find and read these verses in their Bibles: Psalms 12:6; 19:9,10; 119:103,105.

Growing in Obedience

When we know God's Word, it shows in our lives.

Celebration

Feast of Weeks, Firstfruits, Shavuot

Scripture Background

Leviticus 23:15-21

Teacher Materials

Bible with bookmark at Psalm 119:11, samples of different grains (barley, rice, rye, corn, rolled oats, wheat, wheat germ, cracked wheat flour, muesli cereal, puffed oat or rice cereal, etc.).

Bible Verse
I have hidden your word in my heart that I might not sin against you. Psalm 119:11

Introduce the Object Talk

When we know God's Word, it shows in our lives by the good decisions we make and the right actions we take. One of the ways people in Bible times celebrated the Feast of Weeks was by bringing offerings of grains they had grown and harvested. Let's discover how these growing things remind us of obeying God's Word.

Present the Object Talk

1. Show samples of different grains, passing samples around to children and allowing them to taste if desired. (Check for allergies.) **Where do all these kinds of food come from?** (They are grown. You can make bread or cereal from them.) **These are grains. Unlike fruits or vegetables that also grow from the ground, grains are the seeds of plants, mostly different types of grass.**

2. At the Feast of Weeks, also called Shavuot (shah-voo-OHT), the Hebrew word for "weeks,"

God's people celebrated and thanked God for the good things that grow from the earth. When we plant a seed and care for it by giving it light and water, the seed grows and produces grain. When we read and think about God's Word, it grows and produces good things in our lives. What are some of the good things that can grow out of our lives by studying God's Word? (Courage to be honest. Kind ways to treat others. Patience. Knowledge to make good choices.)

Bible Verse
I have hidden your word in my heart that I might not sin against you. Psalm 119:11

Conclude

When we read God's Word and follow what it says, God helps us live the very best way. Read Psalm 119:11 aloud. According to this verse, what should we do to keep from sinning? What do you think it means to hide God's Word in our hearts? (Read God's Word and remember it.) One important thing God's Word tells us about is how to become members of God's family. Talk with children about becoming Christians (see "Leading a Child to Christ" on pp. 16-17). Pray, thanking God for His Word and asking for His help in obeying it.

Discussion Questions

1. **When might kids your age read and think about God's Word?** (When hearing a Bible story at church. When reading a Bible story with parents.)

2. **Who has helped you learn from God's Word?** (Parents. Grandparents. Teachers.)

3. **What do we learn from reading God' Word?** (How to love and obey God. How to show His love to others. How to become members of God's family.)

Additional Information for Older Children

The Feast of Weeks took place at the end of the barley harvest. Because the first sheaf of the barley harvest was to be dedicated, or given, to the Lord, the first day of the Feast of Weeks is called Firstfruits. Read Leviticus 23:9 aloud. Until the dedication was made, no bread, grain or anything from the harvest could be eaten! The people wanted to give God the first and best part of their harvest.

Birthday Candles

God gives us the Holy Spirit to guide us and to help us tell others about Jesus.

Celebration

Pentecost, Trinity Sunday, Birthdays

Scripture Background

Acts 2

Teacher Materials

Bible with bookmark at Acts 28:31, birthday candles; optional—small cake or cupcake, matches.

> **Bible Verse**
> Boldly and without hindrance he preached the kingdom of God and taught about the Lord Jesus Christ. Acts 28:31

Introduce the Object Talk

The Holy Spirit was given to us by God in order to guide us and help us tell others about Jesus. Let's look at a way to remember the special day the Holy Spirit came to the disciples.

Present the Object Talk

1. Display candles you brought. **How are candles used on birthdays? What do the number of candles on a birthday cake often show?** Volunteers tell. (Optional: Place candles in small cake or cupcake. Light candles and allow children to blow them out.)

2. On one day every year, the birthday of God's Church is celebrated. This day is called Pentecost. The word "pentecost" means 50. Pentecost takes place 50

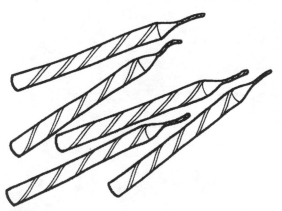

days after the Passover celebration. In Bible times, Jesus' disciples had come to Jerusalem after Jesus had gone to heaven. While they were there, God sent His Holy Spirit to the disciples. This day is celebrated as the beginning of God's Church.

Conclude

The Holy Spirit is still with us, helping us to love and obey God. Read Acts 28:31 aloud. **What does it mean to do something "boldly and without hindrance"?** (To not be afraid. To be brave and confident.) **This verse is talking about Paul. The Holy Spirit helped Paul tell others about Jesus. The Holy Spirit will help us, too! All we have to do is ask.** Pray, thanking God for His gift of the Holy Spirit and asking for His guidance and help as we tell others about Jesus.

Bible Verse

Boldly and without hindrance he preached the kingdom of God and taught about the Lord Jesus Christ. Acts 28:31

Discussion Questions

1. **What happened when God first sent the Holy Spirit?** (The disciples spoke in different languages. Jesus' followers formed the first church.)

2. **Why did God send the Holy Spirit?** (To help members of His family love and obey Him.)

3. **What are some ways the Holy Spirit can help us?** (Guides us in knowing the right things to do. Reminds us of and helps us follow God's commands in the Bible. Helps us know the words to say when we tell others about Jesus.)

Additional Information for Older Children

The first Sunday after Pentecost is called Trinity Sunday. On this day, some churches celebrate the Holy Trinity, the fact that God is made up of three persons: God the Father, God the Son and God the Holy Spirit. One of the objects used to stand for the Holy Trinity is the candle, because a candle is made up of three parts: the wax, the wick and the flame. Children read Jesus' words about the Holy Spirit in John 15:26.

Lighting the Way

Scripture Background

Psalm 59

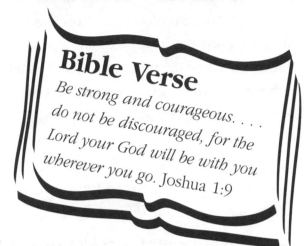

Bible Verse

Be strong and courageous. . . . do not be discouraged, for the Lord your God will be with you wherever you go. Joshua 1:9

Teacher Materials

Bible with bookmarks at Joshua 1:9 and Psalm 59:16,17; object(s) used in dark areas (night-light, flashlight, candle, lantern, etc.); optional—paper, pencils.

Introduce the Object Talk

In all situations, we can count on God to give us the courage we need. Let's look at some things that people might use at times when they are scared.

Present the Object Talk

1. Display object(s) you brought. **What is this? When do people use it? How does it help them?** Volunteers respond. **Sometimes people use these kinds of lights when it's dark. They might need to see where they are going, or maybe they just want to see the light because it makes them feel safe. What are some things younger kids might use to help them feel safe when it's dark?**

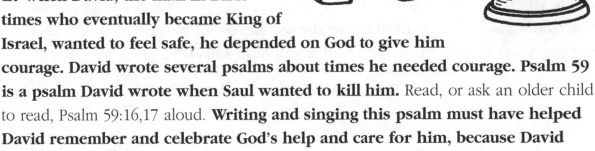

2. When David, the man in Bible times who eventually became King of Israel, wanted to feel safe, he depended on God to give him courage. David wrote several psalms about times he needed courage. Psalm 59 is a psalm David wrote when Saul wanted to kill him. Read, or ask an older child to read, Psalm 59:16,17 aloud. **Writing and singing this psalm must have helped David remember and celebrate God's help and care for him, because David wrote other psalms at other scary times in his life.** (Optional: Children discuss times when they might need God's courage. Lead children to write a group psalm about one of the times mentioned. Read completed psalm aloud with children.)

Conclude

Just as David trusted in God to give him courage, we can also count on God to give us courage in all the situations we face. Read Joshua 1:9 aloud. **Just knowing God is with us wherever we go gives us all the courage we need!** Pray, thanking God for His gift of courage and that He is with us wherever we go.

Bible Verse

Be strong and courageous. . . . do not be discouraged, for the Lord your God will be with you wherever you go. Joshua 1:9

Discussion Questions

1. **What does it mean to have courage?** (To do what is right even when it is hard or we feel afraid.)

2. **When are some times kids your age need courage?** (Taking a test at school. Performing in a music recital or acting in a play. Being around older kids who are mean.)

3. **What can we do to get courage in hard situations?** (Pray to God. Remember God's promise to be with us everywhere we go.)

4. **Why can we always depend on receiving courage from God when we ask for it?** (God always keeps His promises.)

Additional Information for Older Children

In many Bibles, the word *miktam* is written under the title of Psalm 59. No one knows exactly what this word means. Some people think it was a word that described the kind of words David was writing or the melody to which the words were sung. *Miktam* is written under the titles of all the psalms David wrote when he was in great danger. (Optional: Children look at Psalms 56—60.) **Since *miktam* is only written under the psalms David wrote when he was in danger, what do you think the word might have meant?**

Music of Courage

God can give us courage to love our enemies.

Scripture Background
Psalm 57

Teacher Materials
Bible with bookmarks at Psalm 57:8, Psalm 150:3-6 and Luke 6:27; variety of musical instruments (tambourine, cymbals, guitar, autoharp, keyboard, rhythm instruments, etc.); optional—music cassette/CD and player.

> ### Bible Verse
> Love your enemies, do good to those who hate you. Luke 6:27

Introduce the Object Talk
If we pray and ask, God gives us courage to show love to our enemies. In Bible times, people often sang and played instruments to pray for courage or other things. Let's find out about some of the instruments they used.

Present the Object Talk
1. Read, or ask an older child to read, Psalm 150:3-6 while other children count the number of instruments mentioned. **Lyres are like small harps. The way instruments sound often helps us express the feelings of the words we are saying or singing. What kind of feeling would a cymbal make you think of?** Volunteers respond.

2. Psalm 57 is a song written by David at a time when he needed God's courage to love his enemy Saul. Read Psalm 57:8 aloud. **David talked about harps and waking up in the morning. What instruments would remind you of waking up?** Volunteers tell.

3. Distribute instruments to volunteers. **Use these instruments or your hands to make sounds for other phrases in Psalm 57: people chasing someone** (see verse 3), **lions or spears and arrows** (see verse 4), **people falling in a pit** (see verse 6), **a heart constantly beating** (see verse 7). Children experiment with making different sounds. (Optional: Invite a musician to make sounds on an instrument such as an electric guitar or synthesizer.) **At the end of this psalm, David praised God for His love.** (Optional: Play a song for children to accompany with instruments.)

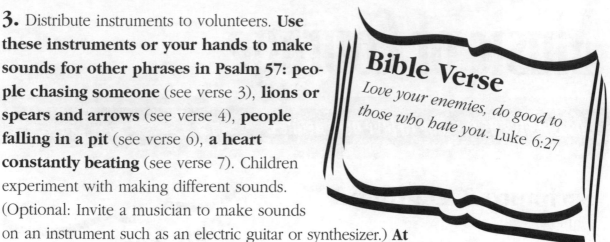

Bible Verse

Love your enemies, do good to those who hate you. Luke 6:27

Conclude

David was able to show God's love, even when Saul didn't deserve it. Read Luke 6:27 aloud. **God has promised that He will give us the courage to do what is right. All we have to do is ask.** Pray, thanking God for His love and asking Him for courage to love everyone, even our enemies.

Discussion Questions

1. What are some ways to show love, and do good things for people you might think of as enemies? (Don't be mean back to them. Don't say mean things about them to others. Smile and be friendly to them.)

2. In what ways can we obey Luke 6:27? (Be kind to others who are mean to us. Pray for people who don't like us. Be kind even when others aren't.)

3. What can you do when it seems too hard to show God's love to an enemy? (Ask God for courage to do what's right. Ask a parent or teacher for advice on how to show love.)

Additional Information for Older Children

Psalm 57 is one of a group of psalms known as the psalms of the history of Israel. Psalms 42 through 72 are about the great deeds God has done for His people, especially those recorded in the book of Exodus. (Optional: Children find and read Psalms 44:1 and 47:1-3 aloud.)

Ties of Love

God shows His love through the actions of people He gives to care for us.

Celebration

Father's Day

Scripture Background

Ephesians 6:1-3

Teacher Materials

Bible with bookmarks at Ephesians 6:1-3 and
1 John 4:11, variety of neckties; optional—one or
more medals.

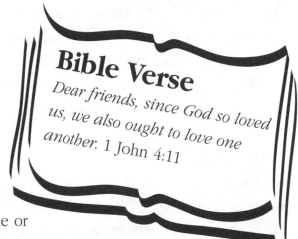

Bible Verse

Dear friends, since God so loved us, we also ought to love one another. 1 John 4:11

Introduce the Object Talk

Through the actions of the people God gives to care for us, we can see His love.
Let's find out about something we can give to honor people who care for us.

Present the Object Talk

1. (Optional: Show one or more medals.) **What kinds of things do people receive
medals for?** (Winning a game or contest. Courageous action in rescuing someone.)
Some medals are called badges of honor. Display neckties you brought. **A necktie
is also a badge of honor. In 1660, King Louis XIV of France saw brightly colored
silk handkerchiefs around the necks of some war heroes from a country called**

**Croatia. He decided to make silk neck-
wear a sign of royalty. Over time, men
everywhere started wearing ties.**
**2. Who do you know who wears
neckties? When are some times you
might give a necktie as a gift? Many
people give their fathers and other
important men in their lives neckties
on Father's Day. The next time you**

give someone a necktie, remember that you are giving a badge of honor for all the ways that this person cares for you! (Optional: Distribute neckties to children and allow them to experiment with tying them around their own necks.)

Bible Verse

Dear friends, since God so loved us, we also ought to love one another. 1 John 4:11

3. Read Ephesians 6:1-3 aloud. **What does this verse say is the right thing to do?** (Obey parents. Honor parents.) **God gave us fathers and other people to love us and take care of us. Who is someone who loves and cares for you? What might you give that person to honor him or her?** Volunteers respond.

Conclude

God loves us so much that He gives us fathers and other people to take care of us. Read 1 John 4:11. **What are some ways you can show love to others? By showing love to others, we are showing our love for God! Loving and caring for others is one of the best ways we can show God's love.** Pray, thanking God for all the people He gives to care for us and asking for His help in showing love to others.

Discussion Questions

1. **How does knowing that God gives us people who care for us make you feel? Why do you think God wants us to have people who care for us?**

2. **What are some ways that fathers care for their children? Who are some people who care for you in this way?**

3. **How can you thank people who care for you? Why do you think these people want to care for you?**

Additional Information for Older Children

When we say the word "father," we are usually talking about our parents. In the Bible, instead of referring only to parents, the word "father" is used as a title of respect for rulers, elders and priests. Children find and read Scriptures about men who were called father as a way of showing respect for them: Joseph—Genesis 45:8; Elijah—2 Kings 2:11,12; Elisha—2 Kings 13:14.

Day of Rest

God gives us a day to rest from work and to worship Him.

Celebration

Sabbath, Shabbot

Scripture Background

Exodus 20:8-11; Leviticus 23:3; Deuteronomy 5:12-18

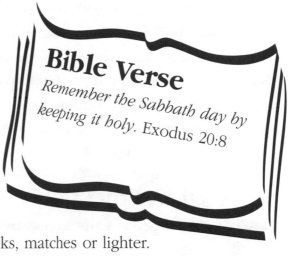

Bible Verse
Remember the Sabbath day by keeping it holy. Exodus 20:8

Teacher Materials

Bible with bookmarks at Exodus 20:8 and Leviticus 23:3, two white candles in candlesticks, matches or lighter.

Introduce the Object Talk

Because He loves us, God gives us a day to rest and worship Him. Let's look at the way people in Bible times celebrated the day of rest, the Sabbath.

Present the Object Talk

1. The Sabbath, the seventh day of the week, was the very first holiday God told His people to celebrate. Read, or ask an older child to read, Leviticus 23:3. **In fact, God was the first to celebrate the Sabbath. What did God do on the seventh day after creating the world?** (He stopped His work and rested.) **The Hebrew word for the Sabbath is *Shabbot* (shah-BAHT), which means "to rest."**

2. Traditionally, God's people worship God together and with their families by celebrating the Sabbath from Friday at sunset to Saturday at sunset. Display candles in candlesticks and light the candles. **At every Sabbath celebration two candles are lit; and prayers, called blessings, are said. The blessings ask God to show His love and care to the people in the family. During the day-long Sabbath, God's people are to rest from all work and take time to celebrate God's love for them—**

especially shown by His creation of the world, His rescue of them from slavery in Egypt and all that He does for His people.

Conclude

Read Exodus 20:8 aloud. **The Sabbath is called holy because it is a special day, a day that is set apart or different from all others. On the Sabbath, we honor and worship God and get the rest we need! Today, Christians all over the world celebrate this day of rest on Sunday, the first day of the week, as a way to joyfully remember that Jesus was raised from the dead on the first day of the week.** Pray, thanking God for His gift of the Sabbath to use to rest and worship Him. Blow out candles.

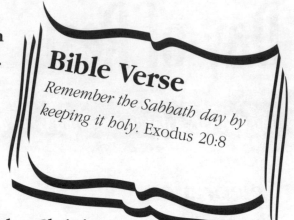

Bible Verse

Remember the Sabbath day by keeping it holy. Exodus 20:8

Discussion Questions

1. **What are some reasons to rest from work and to worship God?** (God knows that everyone needs to rest. To follow God's example of resting. To obey His command to remember the Sabbath.)

2. **What did God create when He made the world? How can we enjoy those things as part of our Sabbath celebration?** (Take a picnic to a forest or park and enjoy the trees and plants God made. Go to a garden and look at the growing things. Go to the zoo and look at all the different types of animals God made. Look at nature books.)

3. **What are some other ways we rest and take time to worship God?** (Stay home from work and school. Go to church. Sing songs to praise God. Visit a sick or lonely person. Show our love for God by obeying Him.)

4. **What's an example of a way your family rests and worships God?** (Read God's Word together. Pray together. Meet with other members of God's family.)

Additional Information for Older Children

Traditionally, two loaves of a braided bread called *challah* (HAH-lah) are eaten at the special Sabbath meal. These two loaves are reminders of the double amount of manna that God provided for the Israelites on the day before the Sabbath while they were traveling in the desert. God gave the extra manna so that the Israelites wouldn't have to work to gather manna on the Sabbath. Children read Exodus 16:22,23. (Optional: Serve *challah* to children.)

Birthdays Around the World

God created us as unique people who can know Him and love one another.

Celebration

Birthdays

Scripture Background

Genesis 1:26-31; 2:4-7,15-23

Teacher Materials

Bible with bookmark at Psalm 100:3, one or more objects used to celebrate birthdays (choose from those listed below).

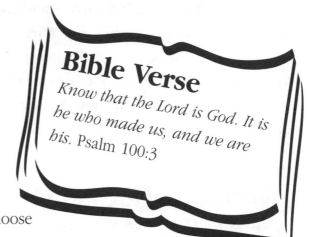

Bible Verse

Know that the Lord is God. It is he who made us, and we are his. Psalm 100:3

Introduce the Object Talk

God created all the people in the world so that we would know Him and love one another. One way we show love to others is by celebrating their birthdays. Let's look at some ways birthdays are celebrated around the world!

Present the Object Talk

1. What do you like to do to celebrate your birthday? Volunteers tell. **Birthdays are good times to show love to people and to celebrate the unique ways in which God made them.**

2. Display and discuss objects you brought that are associated with some of the following birthday traditions: *China*—friends and relatives join in a lunch of noodles to wish the birthday child a long life; *Denmark*—a flag is flown outside a window to show someone in the house is having a birthday; *Japan*—the birthday child wears all new clothes; *Mexico*—the birthday child uses a bat to break open a piñata which is stuffed with candy and small toys to be shared; *Philippines*—blinking lights decorate the home of the birthday child; *Russia*—the birthday child receives a birthday pie with a greeting carved in the crust; *United States*—the birthday child receives a birthday cake with one candle for each year of the child's age. (Optional: Children reenact one or more of the traditions.)

Conclude

Read Psalm 100:3 aloud. **According to this verse, to whom do we belong? Why?** (God. Because He made us.) **God created us and wants us to know and love Him. God also wants us to show His love to others. No matter what the tradition, birthdays are a time to celebrate and show love to people we care about.** Pray, thanking God for creating us and asking His help in loving each other.

Discussion Questions

1. How did God show His love in the ways we are created? (Made our bodies in amazing ways. Gave us minds to think.)

2. What are some ways we can get to know God? (Read the Bible. Listen to older people who love God talk about Him. Ask your parents, pastor or teacher questions about God.)

3. Why should we show love to other people? (To show God's love. Jesus tells us that loving God and loving others are the most important things to do.)

4. What are some ways to show love to other people? (Be kind to them. Help them with tasks they are doing. Care for them when they are upset. Be patient with people who sometimes annoy you.)

Additional Information for Older Children

The most important birthday ever was the day Jesus Christ was born. How did the shepherds celebrate the birth of the baby Jesus? Volunteers answer or children may read Luke 2:16-20. **Who else came to celebrate the birth of Jesus?** (The wise men.) **How did they worship Jesus?** Children tell about the gifts given by wise men or read Matthew 2:9-11.

Group Music

Encourage one another to love and obey God and to do His work.

Scripture Background

Psalm 147

Bible Verse

Encourage one another and build each other up, just as in fact you are doing.
1 Thessalonians 5:11

Teacher Materials

Bible with bookmarks at Psalm 147 and 1 Thessalonians 5:11, paper, photocopier, several CDs/cassettes of different vocal or instrumental groups (duets, trios, choirs, orchestras) and player.

Prepare the Activity

Make five photocopies of Psalm 147:1-5.

Introduce the Object Talk

We can encourage each other to love and obey God and do His work. Let's look at some ways in which people work together to create something wonderful.

Present the Object Talk

1. Briefly play several examples of different types of musical groups. **What is the same about these different types of musical groups? What's different? What do the players or singers need to do in order to make their music sound good?** (Work together to follow the music. Play at the same tempo, or speed. Practice with each other.) **Making music is only one way people work together. What are some other ways?** (Soccer players passing the ball to score a goal. Carpenters building a house.)

2. When there's a big job to be done, it's important to encourage each other to do the job. In Bible times, many people had to work together to rebuild the

wall that had fallen down around Jerusalem. People who study the Bible think that Psalm 147 was written for a choir to sing when the wall was built.

3. Distribute copies of Psalm 147:1-5 to five volunteers. Volunteers read verses in the following manner: One child begins by reading verse one. Another child joins him or her on the second verse. Continue adding voices one at a time until all five volunteers read verse five together. Repeat with new volunteers as time allows.

Bible Verse

Encourage one another and build each other up, just as in fact you are doing.
1 Thessalonians 5:11

Conclude

God gives us other people to help us and encourage us to do His work. Read 1 Thessalonians 5:11 aloud. **When we encourage others, we help them love and obey God.** Pray, thanking God that He gives us people to encourage us, and asking His help to encourage others to love and obey Him and to do His work.

Discussion Questions

1. Why is it important to encourage other people? (It is a way to follow God's command to love one another.)

2. What does it mean to love and obey God and do His work? (Do the things the Bible commands us to do such as love each other; give clothes, money and food to needy people; say kind words to one another instead of arguing; pray for others; etc.)

3. What are some things you could do or say to encourage others to do God's work?

Additional Information for Older Children

Psalm 147 was probably performed by two choirs made up of people called Levites. Levites (people from the tribe of Levi) helped the priests in the Tabernacle and, later, in the Temple. The first choir walked in one direction along the wall while the other choir walked along the wall in the opposite direction! Read about these choirs in Nehemiah 12:27-31,38.

Talented People

Scripture Background

Psalm 145

Teacher Materials

Bible with bookmarks at Psalm 145:10 and
1 Peter 4:10, large sheet of paper, marker,
masking tape; optional—paper, markers.

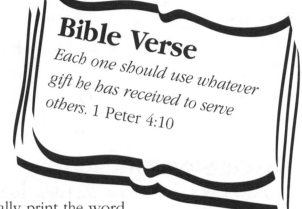

Bible Verse

Each one should use whatever gift he has received to serve others. 1 Peter 4:10

Prepare the Activity

In the middle of large sheet of paper, vertically print the word
"talents," leaving space between each letter. Tape to wall.

Introduce the Object Talk

**Each of us can use the talents God gave us to do good things for others. Let's
talk about different talents and how we can use them in ways that please God.**

Present the Object Talk

1. Show children paper you prepared. **Let's make a kind of acrostic to see how
many talents we can think of that begin with or use each letter of the word
"talents." What are some things that kids your age like to do or are good at?**

Print ideas on large sheet of paper
next to the appropriate letters.
(Optional: Give paper and markers
to children and ask them to make
individual acrostics using their names
and talents.)

**2. Some psalms are written like
acrostics also. Psalm 145 is called
an alphabet acrostic because in
the Hebrew language the verses of**

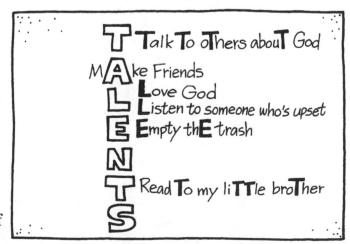

Talk To others abouT God
MAke Friends
Love God
Listen to someone who's upset
Empty thE trash

Read To my liTTle broTher

the psalm begin with the letters of the Hebrew alphabet in order. King David wrote this psalm a long time ago. In this psalm we can read a reason we have all been given special talents. Read, or ask a child to read, Psalm 145:10. **When we use our talents to help others, it's a way of serving and praising God.**

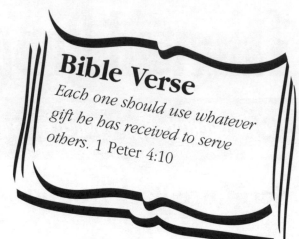

Conclude

Read 1 Peter 4:10 aloud. **What does it mean to serve others?** (To help them. To give them what they need.) **What are some ways kids your age can serve others?** Pray, thanking God for the talents He's given us and asking for His help in finding ways to use our talents to help others.

Discussion Questions

1. **How has someone used a talent to help you?** (Helped me learn to read. Helped me make friends.)

2. **What kinds of things do you enjoy doing? What are you good at doing?** (Being friendly. Playing soccer. Reading. Singing.)

3. **When have you used a talent to serve others?**

Additional Information for Older Children

Read, or ask an older child to read, Romans 12:6-8 aloud. **What are some of the talents, or gifts, this verse describes?** Volunteers respond. **In this verse, the word "gift" comes from the Greek word *charismata* (kah-rees-MAH-tah). This word tells us these gifts are special, freely given by God to meet the needs of His family.**

Cheerful Praise

Use your abilities to give praise to God.

Scripture Background

Psalm 136

Teacher Materials

Bible with bookmark at Psalm 136, objects used to cheer sports teams (pom poms, pennants, large foam fingers, etc.).

Bible Verse

Give thanks to the Lord, for he is good. His love endures forever. Psalm 136:1

Introduce the Object Talk

We can give praise to God when we use the abilities and talents He gave us. Let's look at a way people praised God in Old Testament times.

Present the Object Talk

1. When a sports team scores a goal, what does the crowd do? (Cheers.) Display objects used to cheer sports teams. (Optional: **What are some of your favorite cheers?** Lead children in a few cheers—"Give me an A!" "We've got spirit; yes, we do!" "2, 4, 6, 8! Who do we appreciate?")

2. Because God is so good to us and because He loves us so much, we want to cheer for joy! One meaning of the word "cheer" is to praise someone or something. The book of Psalms is a book of praise songs. The writers of the psalms used their abilities and talents to praise God.

3. Psalm 136 is a psalm written in an interesting way. After each sentence said by the Old Testament song leader, the choir or worshipers would say "His love endures forever." What does it mean when the psalm says "His love endures forever"? (It will never end. God will always love us.) Lead a reading of Psalm 136 in the manner described (i.e., read, or ask an older child to read, the verses and lead children in saying the refrain "His love endures forever").

Bible Verse
Give thanks to the Lord, for he is good. His love endures forever. Psalm 136:1

Conclude

Because God loves us so much, He gives us abilities that we can use to celebrate and praise Him. Pray, thanking God for the abilities He gives us.

Discussion Questions

1. **How have you seen people at church use their abilities to praise God?** (Make banners. Sing songs. Play music.)

2. **What are some things kids your age can do to praise God? What abilities do you have that you could use to praise and worship God?**

3. **Why do you think praising God is important?**

Additional Information for Older Children

When things are scary or difficult, it may seem hard to praise God. But in the Old Testament, we can read about King Jehoshaphat and how he praised God even when three different armies were coming against his country! To show that they believed God's promise to fight the battle for them, the king and his people chose singers to lead the army instead of soldiers! The singers didn't carry swords—they carried cymbals and harps and other instruments! Read what happened in 2 Chronicles 20:20-22.

Praise Parade

Scripture Background

Psalm 24

Teacher Materials

Bible with bookmarks at Psalm 24 and
Psalm 149:1, large sheet of paper, marker,
masking tape; optional—objects used at
parades (serpentine rolls, confetti, balloons,
batons, whistles, drums, etc.).

Bible Verse

Praise the Lord. Sing to the Lord a new song, his praise in the assembly of the saints. Psalm 149:1

Prepare the Activity

On the large sheet of paper, draw one line for each letter of the name of several
objects used at parades (see suggested list above). (Optional: Use objects associated
with specific parades in your community.) Tape paper to wall.

Introduce the Object Talk

**When God's family gets together, we celebrate
and praise God! Let's look at one way big
crowds of people get together and
celebrate special occasions.**

Present the Object Talk

1. Display paper you prepared. Invite volunteers to
suggest letters of the alphabet. As volunteers suggest letters,
print letters on the correct lines. If a letter is not used in any
of the words you are using, write the letter at the bottom of
the paper. As letters fill in the words, children guess what the
words are. **All of these words are the names of things used
at a special event. Guess what the event is!** Volunteers respond
until the event, a parade, is revealed.

2. Another word like "parade" is "procession." A procession is a group of people moving forward together, usually as part of a very special ceremony. Processions are an important part of funerals, graduations and weddings. Often, music accompanies processions. Psalm 24 is a song that was written for the procession David led when he brought the Ark of the Covenant to Jerusalem. (The Ark was a special box that reminded the people of God's presence.) Read, or ask an older child to read, Psalm 24:7-10 aloud. (Optional: As verses are read, children walk in a procession around the room.)

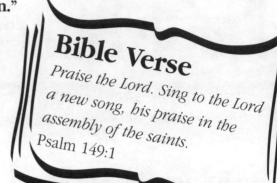

Bible Verse
Praise the Lord. Sing to the Lord a new song, his praise in the assembly of the saints.
Psalm 149:1

Conclude

When David brought the Ark to Jerusalem, the Israelites celebrated and praised God. As members of God's family, we can celebrate and praise God, too! Read Psalm 149:1 aloud. **An assembly is a large group of people. When are some times large groups of people come together to praise God?** Pray, thanking God that the members of His family can celebrate and praise Him together.

Discussion Questions

1. What has God given you to show His love for you? Volunteers respond. **How has God given you courage? When has God forgiven you?**

2. Why is it important to celebrate these gifts God gives us? (To recognize God's constant goodness to His people. To remember the good gifts God gives us every day.)

3. What are some ways to praise God with other members of His family?

4. What is one way you can praise God with your family this week? (Sing a praise song together before eating dinner. Each person in the family thanks God for something when you pray together. Together, make a poster telling God reasons you love Him.)

Additional Information for Older Children

Many psalms were written for special occasions. Psalm 132 may have been written for two occasions: the Temple dedication (children compare Psalm 132:8-10 to 2 Chronicles 6:41,42) **and when the king was crowned** (children read Psalm 132:18).

The Bells Are Ringing

When we talk to God, we can worship Him for who He is and what He has done.

Celebration
Call to Worship, Invocation

Scripture Background
Psalm 100

Teacher Materials
Bible with bookmarks at Psalm 100 and Daniel 2:20, bell(s); optional—pictures of bells.

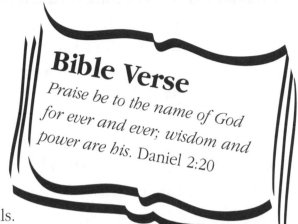

Bible Verse
Praise be to the name of God for ever and ever; wisdom and power are his. Daniel 2:20

Introduce the Object Talk
For all that God is and all that He has done, we can worship God by talking to Him. Let's look at a way to know that it is time to come together and worship God.

Present the Object Talk
1. Display bell(s) you brought. (Optional: Show pictures of bells.) Allow volunteers to ring the bell(s). **Bells often tell people when it's time to do something. What kinds of bells can you think of that tell you it's time for something?** (School bells. Dinner bells. Customer-service bells. Emergency Broadcast System warning bells. Church bells.) **Many churches have bell towers and bells that are rung to let people know it is time for a worship service.**

2. When God's followers come together, they sometimes read verses from the Bible that tell everyone it's time to worship God. The verses that are read are called a call to worship. Psalm 100 is a call to worship. Ask older volunteers to read the psalm, one verse at a time. **The words of this psalm help people think about how**

and why we should worship God. At the beginning and end of the psalm, as well as at the end of each verse, invite volunteers to ring the bell(s) as another reminder to worship God.

Bible Verse

Praise be to the name of God for ever and ever; wisdom and power are his. Daniel 2:20

Conclude

When Daniel lived in Bible times, he worshiped God, too. Read Daniel 2:20 aloud. **What two words does this verse use to describe God?** ("Wisdom" and "power.") **What are some of the ways God's wisdom and power help people today?** (Answer our prayers. Give us courage. Help us do right.) Pray, thanking God and praising Him for His wisdom and power.

Discussion Questions

1. **Who are some people who often receive praise in our world today?** (Athletes. Movie stars.) **Why is it important to worship and praise God?** (Because God is greater than anyone else, He deserves our worship and praise. We want to tell God we love Him and how glad we are about all the things He has done for us.)

2. **In Psalm 100, the words "gates" and "courts" are referring to places in the Temple where people worshiped God in Bible times. Where are some places that we could enter, giving thanks and praise to God?** (Church. Home. School.)

3. **What does Psalm 100 mean by describing God as faithful to all generations (a generation is a group of people born at the same time)?** (God has cared for people and loved people all through the history of the world.)

4. **What do you want to praise God for today?** Tell your own answer to this question before inviting volunteers to answer.

Additional Information for Older Children

Many psalms have the words "of David" written at the beginning of the psalm. This phrase could mean that David wrote the psalm or that the psalm was written by someone else and dedicated to David. Look at these psalms to find who Bible scholars think either wrote the psalm or used the psalm in worship.

Children look at these psalms to find the probable authors: Psalm 19 (David, king of Israel); Psalm 42 (the sons of Korah, a group of musicians); Psalm 50 (Asaph, a choir leader in David's time); Psalm 90 (Moses, leader of God's people when they escaped from Egypt).

Light Lesson

Celebrations

Transfiguration Sunday

Scripture Background

Matthew 17:1-13; Luke 9:28-36

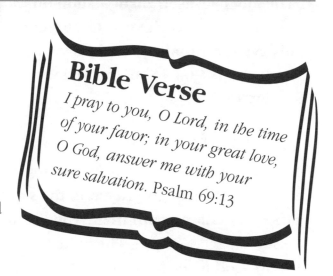

Bible Verse
I pray to you, O Lord, in the time of your favor; in your great love, O God, answer me with your sure salvation. Psalm 69:13

Teacher Materials

Bible with bookmarks at Matthew 17:2 and Psalm 69:13, sheet of white paper, marker, flashlight or lamp with bare bulb.

Prepare the Activity

Fold paper in half. Draw a sun on folded paper.

Introduce the Object Talk

We can get to know Jesus, God's Son, when we pray. One time when three of Jesus' disciples were praying with Him, they learned that Jesus was God's Son. Let's find out what happened.

Present the Object Talk

1. Holding paper so that drawing faces you, shine light from flashlight or lamp directly on the blank side of the paper. **When I shine this light directly on the sheet of paper, what do you see?** (Nothing but the paper.) Without moving paper, move light source behind paper. **When I shine the light from behind the paper, what do you see?** (The sun drawn on the paper.)

2. **The Bible tells us about a time when light made Jesus' disciples see Him in a different way. His face shone as bright as the sun and**

made them know He was God's Son. Jesus' appearance changed so much that the Bible says He was transfigured. The word "transfigure" means to change. Read, or ask an older child to read, Matthew 17:2. **Many churches remember Jesus' transfiguration on a special Sunday each year. Celebrating this event reminds God's followers that Jesus is God's Son, the Savior sent by God.**

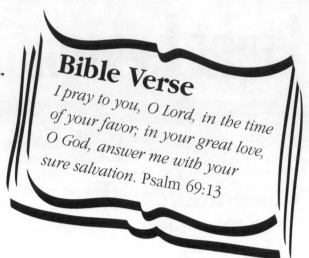

Bible Verse

I pray to you, O Lord, in the time of your favor; in your great love, O God, answer me with your sure salvation. Psalm 69:13

Conclude

We can get to know Jesus by reading about Him in the Bible. We also get to know Jesus through prayer. In the same way you become better friends with others by talking with them, you get to know Jesus better whenever you pray. Read Psalm 69:13 aloud. **The writer of this verse is praying to God because he knows God loves him and will answer his prayers.** Pray, thanking God for Jesus, His Son, and asking God's help in getting to know who Jesus is. Talk with children about becoming Christians. Follow the guidelines in the "Leading a Child to Christ" article on pages 16-17.

Discussion Questions

1. **What are some things you know about Jesus?** (He is God's Son. He loves us. He is always with us.) **How have you gotten to know who Jesus is?** (From teachers and parents. From reading God's Word.)

2. **Why do you think praying helps us get to know Jesus?** (When we pray, it reminds us of Jesus' love and care for us.)

3. **What kinds of things can you talk to Jesus about?**

4. **When are some times you pray every day? When are some other times you can pray?**

Additional Information for Older Children

About a week prior to Jesus' transfiguration on the mountain, Jesus asked His disciples who people thought He was. Jesus also asked who THEY thought He was. Read what Peter said in Matthew 16:13-16.

Worldwide Prayer

We can learn the best way to pray from Jesus' examples.

Celebration

The Lord's Prayer

Scripture Background

Matthew 6:9-13

Teacher Materials

Bible with bookmarks at Matthew 6:9
and Philippians 4:6, large sheet of
paper, marker; optional—globe or world map,
flags from countries listed below (pictures of flags may be found
in encyclopedias or on the Internet).

Bible Verse

Do not be anxious about anything, but in everything, by prayer and petition, with thanksgiving, present your requests to God. Philippians 4:6

Prepare the Activity

On large sheet of paper, print one or more of the following: Spanish—*Nuestro Padre en el cielo* (nyoo-EH-stroh PAH-dreh een ehl see-EH-loh); French—*Notre Père dans le ciel* (NOH-treh PEHR dahn leh SEE-ehl); German—*Unser Vater in Himmel* (OON-suhr VAH-tuhr ihn HIHM-uhl); Tagalog (Philippines)—*Ama Namin sumasa-langit ka* (Ah-mah NAH-meen soo-MAH-sah LAHN-geet kah); Norwegian—*Våre Far inne himmelen* (VAHR FAHR IHN-eh HIH-meh-lehn); Afrikaans (South Africa)—*Ons Vader in hemel* (AHNS VAH-duhr ihn HIHM-uhl); Kwazulu (South Africa)—*Ubaba Wethu Ebhakabhaka* (OO-bah-bah WEE-thoo EHB-hah-kahb-hah-kah). Practice saying the phrases.

Norway

South Africa

Introduce the Object Talk

When Jesus lived on earth, He taught us how to talk to God. One prayer that Jesus prayed, called the Lord's Prayer, is prayed by people all over the world. Let's find out about some of the first words in this prayer and practice saying them in different languages.

Present the Object Talk

1. When Jesus taught the disciples to pray, what name did He use for God? Read Matthew 6:9 aloud. **Jesus was speaking in the Aramaic language and the word He used for Father was** *Abba* **(AH-bah).** *Abba* **actually means "Daddy"! Jesus showed how much He was loved by His Father in heaven by calling Him Daddy.**

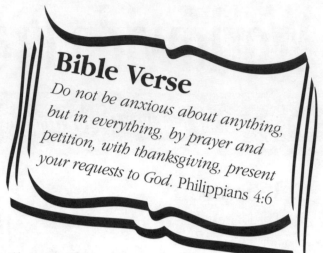

Bible Verse

Do not be anxious about anything, but in everything, by prayer and petition, with thanksgiving, present your requests to God. Philippians 4:6

2. Jesus' example shows us that can talk to God as our Daddy, too. People in each country of the world say the words of the Lord's Prayer in their own languages. Show paper you prepared. **This is how people say "Our Father in heaven" in (Spanish).** Repeat for each language. Include volunteers in your group who speak other languages. (Optional: Show map or globe and identify locations of countries, or show flags or pictures of flags you have collected.)

Conclude

Read Philippians 4:6. **The word "anxious" means worried. What should we do instead of worry?** (Talk to God.) Ask children to thank God for His gift of prayer, inviting them to begin with "Our Father in heaven" in any of the languages written on large sheet of paper.

Discussion Questions

1. What are some things Jesus prayed about? What did Jesus ask His Father in heaven to do?

2. What are some things kids your age worry about?

3. How do you think talking to God about your worries will help? (God will listen to you. He will give you courage. God will remind you that He is with you. God always answers prayer in the very best way.)

4. What are some things you can thank and praise God for? What are some things you need God to help you with?

Additional Information for Older Children

When Jesus prayed at Gethsemane on the night He was betrayed by Judas, He again began His prayer with the Aramaic word *Abba.* **Read this prayer in Mark 14:35,36.**

120

The End Is Just the Beginning

God's gifts to us make it possible for us to worship Him in everything we do and obey Him in all situations so that others may come to know and love Him.

Scripture Background

Psalm 67

Teacher Materials

Bible with bookmark at Psalm 67:1,2; objects from graduations (pictures, mortarboard, diploma, etc.).

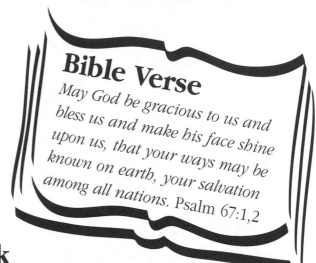

Bible Verse

May God be gracious to us and bless us and make his face shine upon us, that your ways may be known on earth, your salvation among all nations. Psalm 67:1,2

Introduce the Object Talk

Others may come to know and love God when we worship and obey Him in all situations. Let's talk about a time in our lives that may seem like the end but that is also a beginning.

Present the Object Talk

1. Have you ever been to a graduation? What are some of the things you saw there? Show objects you brought. Ask volunteers to identify objects and explain how they are used at a graduation.

What do you think is the reason for a graduation cele-  **bration?** Volunteers respond. **Some people think of a graduation only as the end of something—the end of going to a particular school. But a graduation is also a time to begin something new—the beginning of a new school, for example, or a job.**

2. At the end of most worship services, a pastor or church leader will usually say a prayer called a benediction. A benediction is something good that is spoken to people to help people remember that God is with them even after the worship service is over. Reading or singing a benediction not only means that the worship service is ended, but it also means that now we can begin the new

week loving and obeying God with the gifts He has given us. Read or ask an older child to read the benediction in Psalm 67:1,2. (Optional: Lead children in singing the song or saying the words that your church uses as a benediction at worship services.)

Bible Verse

May God be gracious to us and bless us and make his face shine upon us, that your ways may be known on earth, your salvation among all nations. Psalm 67:1,2

Conclude

Prayers or songs of benediction remind us that even though the worship service is ending, we can begin the new week worshiping God every day as we love and obey Him. God's gifts to us make it possible for us to love Him and help others become part of His family, too. Talk with children about becoming members of God's family, following the guidelines in the "Leading a Child to Christ" article (see pp. 16-17). Pray, asking for God's help to love and obey Him in all situations.

Discussion Questions

1. **What are some of the gifts God has given members of His family?** (His love and care. Prayer. Other people who believe in and love Jesus.)

2. **In what ways can kids your age show that they want to love and obey God?**

3. **How can we help others become members of God's family?** (Care for them. Pray for them.)

Additional Information for Older Children

The word "benediction" comes from the Latin *bene* **("good") and** *dicuts* **("speaking"). This tells us that the benediction is a blessing pronounced over everyone present, asking God to bless the hearers with help and strength as the new week begins. A benediction may also be a blessing to God, praising Him for His goodness.**

Index

God's Gifts

Care

Courage

Creation (Abilities)

Forgiveness

God's Family

Guidance

Jesus

Love

Power

Prayer

Promises

Salvation

Wisdom

Holidays

Scripture Reference

Bible Verse

Smart Resources for Your Children's Ministry

unday School Smart Pages
raining, inspiration, materials,
uick solutions and more for
eaching ages 2 to 12.
eproducible
Manual • ISBN 08307.15215

Sunday School Promo Pages
Resources and advice to recruit
teachers, gain church support,
increase attendance and more.
Reproducible
Manual • ISBN 08307.15894

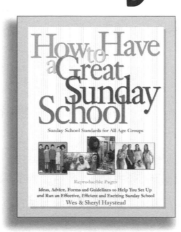

**How to Have a Great
Sunday School**
Ideas, advice, forms and guidelines
to help you set up and run an
effective, efficient and exciting
Sunday School at every age level.
Reproducible
Manual • ISBN 08307.18265

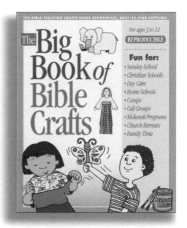

The Big Book of Bible Crafts
Fun for Sunday School,
Christian Schools, Day Care,
Home Schools, Cell Groups,
Midweek Programs, and
Family Time. Ages 3 to 12.
Reproducible
Manual • ISBN 08307.25733

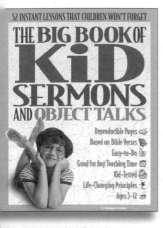

**The Big Book of Kid
Sermons and Object Talks**
2 instant lessons! Everyday
bjects are used to illustrate
fe-changing principles of the
Bible for kids to understand.
Ages 5 to 12.
Reproducible
Manual • ISBN 08307.25164

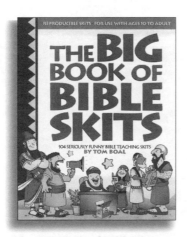

The Big Book of Bible Skits
104 seriously funny Bible teaching
skits. Includes discussion questions.
Ages 10 to adult.
Reproducible
Manual • ISBN 08307.19164

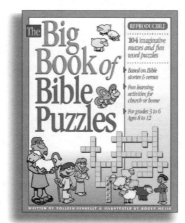

The Big Book of Bible Puzzles
104 imaginative mazes and
fun word puzzles based on Bible
stories and verses. Fun learning
activites for grades 3 to 6. Ages 8
to 12.
Reproducible
Manual • ISBN 08307.25423

The Big Book of Bible Games
200 fun games that teach Bible
concepts and life application.
Ages 5 to 12.
Reproducible
Manual • ISBN 08307.18214

Available at your local Christian bookstore.
www.gospellight.com

Gospel Light
God's Word for a Kid's World!

41776